The Complete SEO 2015 & Beyond

SEO 2015 & Beyond + An SEO Checklist

By Dr. Andy Williams

http://ezseonews.com

Version 4.0

8th December 2015

The Complete SEO 2015 & Beyond

Includes: SEO 2015 & Beyond + An SEO Checklist

This book contains my 2 popular SEO books in a single **volume:**

SEO 2015 & Beyond

Search Engine Optimization will never be the same again

Google Panda seems to penalize low quality content, whereas Penguin is more concerned about overly aggressive SEO tactics. Stuff that SEOs had been doing for years, not only doesn't work anymore, but now can cause your site to be penalized and drop out of the rankings. Just about everything you have been taught about SEO in the last 10 years can be thrown out the Window. Google have moved the goal posts. In this book, I want to share with you the new SEO, the SEO for 2015 & Beyond.

SEO Checklist

A step-by-step plan for fixing SEO problems with your web site.

It provides a step-by-step plan to fix a broken site and contains detailed checklists with an explanation of why those things are important. These checklists are based on the SEO that I use on a daily basis. It's the SEO I teach my students, and it's the SEO that I know works. For those that embrace the recent changes, SEO has actually become easier as we no longer have to battle against other sites whose SEO was done 24/7 by an automated tool or an army of cheap labor. Those sites have largely been removed, and that levels the playing field. If you have a site that lost rankings, this book gives you a step-by-step action plan and checklist to fix problems that are common causes of ranking penalties.

Contents
BOOK 1 - SEO 2015 & Beyond

Book 2 - An SEO Checklist

SEO

2015 & Beyond

Search engine optimization will never be the same again!

By Dr. Andy Williams

ezSEONews
Creating Fat Content

4th Major Version

Released: 8th December 2014

What people said about the previous versions of this book

"Read this book and anything else you can get your hands on by this guy."

"Dr. Andy Williams is to my mind the man to listen to when it comes to the subject of building a website in a clean ethical manner. His explanations of what Google and the other search engines consider as part of the ranking process cannot be bettered. If you wish to create a long lived website that does not need to fear the latest Google update(s) then pay heed." **Jim**

"After 10 years online building and promoting websites, I became quite adept at SEO (both on-page and off), but that was then, and this is now! Having read this eBook from cover to cover, I think you would be hard pressed to find more informative, descriptive, and easy-to-understand material on the subject of present day SEO anywhere." **Andy Aitch**

"This is the right way to build websites. There is a slot of rubbish written by many so-called experts, but this is not one of them. If you want to learn the best way to do SEO, then this is the leading book I have read, and I have read many." **Dobsy "Dobsy" (UK)**

"Basically I loved this book and highly recommend it. It is the best couple bucks you will ever spend. It is easy to read, succinct, and brilliant. He offers a lot of great tips without all the fluff that some authors throw in to add page count. Thanks Andy for a good read that upped my SEO IQ." **Nicole Bernd**

"Since Penguin was released in April 2012, SEO has been turned on its head. Creating themed content with LSI in mind, instead of keyword focused content, is now the way to go.

Amazingly, this is exactly what Andy has been teaching for the past ten years. I only wished I had known him when I started out in internet marketing as his style of teaching is the best. He's a very genuine and generous person and if you've been hit by Panda or Penguin, this book is exactly what you need." **Carole**

"Great book, super helpful and makes seo easy to understand, especially for ecommerce novice! Would definitely recommend to anyone trying to get a handle on best practices in seo." **cswaff**

"He was warning of a Panda type hit at least two years before the Panda was born. Although the Penguin has changed things more than a bit, in this book, Dr

Andy clearly, and in simple terminology, explains the strategies and tactics needed to stay on the good side of Google." **Tony Crofts**

"Great at teaching the difference in old SEO practices vs. New techniques." **Ms. WriterGirl**

"Andy is one of the few people that I listen to when it comes to SEO because rather than "follow the usual crowd", that tends to share rehashed information with little value that's based on fact, he does his own testing to determine what is actually working for him, and then shares his own results." **J. Stewart**

"This book was a very quick and easy read from start to finish. I found it to be an excellent work with some very mature insight into the nuances of how to get in good graces with Google. It took a few of my beliefs and approaches to Search Engine Optimization and turned them upside down." **Jonathan W. Walker**

"This is ground breaking Internet marketing information. Stuff you won't find elsewhere. Being a longtime pupil of Dr. Andy, I have put much of it to the test myself and I know it proves out. If you are in the Internet business, you need to read this book." **Norman Morrison**

"After following Andy Williams for over 8 years now I had a hunch his new SEO, 2013 & Beyond would be a winner . . . and it is. Simple, straight forward and on target with respect to the latest updates, upgrades, and algorithmic mods by our friends at Google. Do what Andy teaches, especially with reference to great content creation, and you will be successful in your SEO efforts." **Chris Cobb**

DISCLAIMER AND TERMS OF USE AGREEMENT

The author and publisher of this eBook and the accompanying materials have used their best efforts in preparing this eBook. The author and publisher make no representation or warranties with respect to the accuracy, applicability, fitness, or completeness of the contents of this eBook. The information contained in this eBook is strictly for educational purposes. Therefore, if you wish to apply ideas contained within this eBook, you are taking full responsibility for your actions.   The author and publisher disclaim any warranties (express or implied), merchantability, or fitness for any particular purpose. The author and publisher shall in no event be held liable to any party for any direct, indirect, punitive, special, incidental or other consequential damages arising directly or indirectly from any use of this material, which is provided "as is", and without warranties. The author and publisher do not warrant the performance, effectiveness or applicability of any sites listed or linked to in this eBook. All links are for information purposes only and are not warranted for content, accuracy or any other implied or explicit purpose. The author and publisher of this book are not in any way associated with Google. This eBook is © copyrighted by Lunasoft Marketing, SL and is protected under the US Copyright Act of 1976 and all other applicable international, federal, state and local laws, with ALL rights reserved. No part of this may be copied, or changed in any format, sold, or used in any way other than what is outlined within this eBook under any circumstances without express permission from Lunasoft Marketing, SL

A note about Page rank

If you have never heard of Page Rank before, let me give you a quick introduction.

Every page on the internet has something called Page Rank (also called PR). PR is measured on a logarithmic scale from 0 to 10. A new page will have a PR of 0. Actually it won't be zero, but very close.

When page A links to page B, page B gets an increase in its PR that is a proportion of the PR on page A.

If page A has a PR of zero, page B gets very little additional PR. If page A has a PR of 5, page B gets a huge boost in its PR.

If a page has a lot of incoming links, it gathers PR from each of those pages, making it more "important". This is where we get the idea of a link being a vote for a page. The more links a page has, the more PR it has and the more important it is. The more important a page, the easier it will rank in the Google SERPs.

For many years, PR has been discussed and talked about in SEO circles like some ranking Deity. PR was seen as an all-powerful property of a page that could be sculpted and used to make other pages rank better.

PR showed how important a page was. That's importance to Google!

Google even provided a toolbar for webmasters to check the PR for any page:

https://support.google.com/toolbar/answer/79837?hl=en

For many webmasters, SEO became a game of chasing PR. Getting links on high PR pages was the only thing that mattered.

By giving webmasters the toolbar, Google gave them the power to rank at will, funneling and sculpting PR to important pages to give them the ranking power to dominate the SERPs.

However, for the last couple of years, Google has been trying to distance itself from PR, trying to convince webmasters that it was no longer an important factor. Google even stopped updating their toolbar so no one could tell the true PR of a page. The last update I am aware of was in December 2013.

In October 2014, Google's John Mueller said "We are probably not going to be updating it [PageRank] going forward, at least in the Toolbar PageRank.".

Clearly that "...at least in the Toolbar PageRank" statement indicates PR is still important to Google. They just don't want webmasters knowing the PR of pages as it gives them too much control.

While we do talk about PR a little in this book, there is no emphasis on it. PR is important in the way it is accrued (because a page with high PR has a lot of good links pointing to it, and is therefore an important page) but it is no longer that SEO deity. With that being said, let's get started.

What is SEO?

SEO stands for **S**earch **E**ngine **O**ptimization and can be defined as the steps a webmaster takes to increase the visibility of his/her pages in the search engine's organic search results.

We should really define a couple of terms at this point.

A **webmaster** is simply a person that is responsible for a particular website.

Organic search results are those listings in the SERPs that are there on merit because of their relevance to the search term that was typed in. It's important to differentiate between organic and paid listings. With paid listings, webmasters pay the search engines to have their pages listed at the top.

In the last paragraph, I used the term **SERPs**. This refers to the **S**earch **E**ngine **R**esults **P**ages. In other words, the pages of results you get when you carry out a search at a search engine.

Before we go any further, I should mention that this book focuses on Google SEO. Google is the largest search engine on the planet and most search traffic around the world comes from Google. Google has become synonymous with the term search engine, and it has even found its way into the English dictionary as a verb. I expect you've heard someone describe how they **googled** something or other. Google is the most important place to rank well, and if you rank well there, chances are you will rank well on Yahoo and Bing too.

Why is SEO necessary?

So you want to build a website, huh?

Unfortunately if you build it, they won't come, at least not without some help from the search engines. The sad truth is that you can have the best website on the planet, but if people cannot find it, it will be a very lonely place. And that brings us back to search engines.

Search engines are the #1 way people find websites.

The good news is that it is easy to get your pages into the search engines.

The bad news is that it is difficult to get your pages to rank high enough to be visible in the search engines.

A study based on data from July 2014 showed that the page that ranks in position #1 of the SERPS, typically gets around 31% of all clicks.

The web page ranked in position #2 gets 14%.

The page in #3 gets 10%.

If we look at position 6 to 10 combined, they get around 3.7% of the clicks.

Web pages ranked on page 2 of the results get around 4% of clicks, and on page 3+, it drops to 1.6% of clicks.

From this information, you can see that it is important to not only rank in Google, but to rank as highly as possible. Even one or two places can mean big drops in potential traffic.

You can read the full report here:

http://www.advancedwebranking.com/google-ctr-study-2014.html

How do we rank pages as high as possible?

To rank high in the organic search results, your page needs to be one of the best matches for the search term typed into the search engine.

What makes a page the best match?

Well that is a secret known only to Google, but a little later in this chapter we'll look at some of the factors Google consider when ranking web pages.

How we used to rank pages

In the good old days (that's up to about 2010), ranking in Google was easy.

You see at the time, Google's algorithm (the complex code that determines where a webpage will rank) was heavily based on the keywords on a page and the links from other websites pointing to that page. Webmasters discovered this, and since both of those factors could be controlled and manipulated by the webmaster, they began controlling and manipulating.

Here was the process:

1. Identify keywords we wanted to rank for.
2. Create a page that was optimized for that keyword. The quality of the content was not important. What was important was that you stuffed your chosen keyword into as many places as possible. The title of the page, the opening header, in the body of the content maybe 5 times per 100 words, in ALT tags for images and image names. Maybe even in the domain name itself. The more times you could get your term in there, the better.
3. Build backlinks by the thousands using automated backlinking tools. The anchor text for most of the backlinks was the same as the term(s) we wanted to rank for.

That was it. You could rank for literally any term using that simple formula.

Webmasters were able to rank anything they wanted, for whatever they wanted. Google had lost control.

As you can imagine, the SERPs became very poor quality, and that made Google look bad. Google wanted the best, most relevant results to be shown to searchers. In many cases, spots in the top 10 were filled with very poor quality content.

Over time, Google has refined its algorithm making it more and more difficult for webmasters to game the system. In Google's ideal world, their prized algorithm would be based entirely on factors that webmasters could not control or manipulate.

As we'll see later in the book, Google's Panda and Penguin (as well as several other major updates) were designed to start taking the control back from webmasters. By removing the factors that webmasters could control from their algorithm, or giving them less importance, Google made it increasingly difficult to manipulate a web page ranking. When we look at the top ranking factors in 2015 (later in this chapter), bear this in mind.

Personalized Search Results

In recent years, Google has been applying more and more personalization to the search results. That means, what you see when you search for a phrase in Google may not be the same as someone in a different part of the country would see for the same search term. In fact, it may not be the same set of results your neighbour sees, or your mom sitting next to you on the couch while searching on her mobile phone.

It is important to realize this. Not everyone sees the same results.

When someone searches at Google, the search giant will apply filters to the results in an attempt to show that searcher the most relevant results based on their personal circumstances.

As a quick example, if you search Google for an antivirus program while using your iMac, you'll probably see a bias of anti-virus pages in the SERPs targeting Mac users.

Do the same search on a PC and you'll get PC antivirus software.

Repeat the search on an Android phone or iPhone, and you'll get results tailored to those operating systems.

That is just a simple example. Google looks at more than just the operating system. Other factors they'll try to use include:

- Your location (whether that is your reported location, IP address or GPS location reported by mobile devices).

- Your search history. What have you been searching for in recent days?
- Your social networks, your likes, friends and circles.
- Whether you are searching on a mobile, desktop or even SmartTV.
- Your preferred language.

Personalization of results is meant to make our lives easier, and in many ways it does. However, as an SEO, it can be a pain if we don't know what other people are seeing in the SERPs.

Top Ranking Factors in 2015

Earlier we said that Google wanted to build its algorithm around quality indicators that are not under webmaster control. In this section, we'll look at some of the indicators used by Google. Think about each one, and how much control a webmaster has over each one.

Ranking Factors can be split into two groups – "on page" and "off page".

On Page Factors

1. Quality Content

Google is looking for high quality content that is relevant to the search query. They'll look at the language used on the page, and for terms related to the query. I call these theme words. Longer pages tend to do better, and the inclusion of photos and/or video works to your advantage if they help to retain the visitor's interest.

2. Fast loading of the page

Nobody likes waiting around for a page to load. If your web pages are taking 5 or more seconds, your visitors may decide not to wait and hit the back button. If they came from Google, that is bad news for you, since Google sees the "bounce" as a negative thing related to your page.

3. Internal links from other pages on the site.

If you look at a website like Wikipedia, you'll see a lot of **internal links**. Internal links are simply pages on a site linking to other pages on the same site. Any links we talk about in this book that link out to other websites will be called **external links**. Internal links are there to help the visitor. As someone reads a page on Wikipedia, they might come across a word or phrase they do not understand (or simply want to know more about). By "internally" linking key words or phrases to another pages on Wikipedia, visitors can navigate around the site and get the information they are looking for.

4. Bounce rates

We mentioned bounce rates earlier in the context of fast loading pages. A bounce is simply a visitor that clicks a link in the SERPs and then returns to Google. The quicker the return, the worse it is for your page as it tells Google the visitor was not satisfied.

Let's think how this might work.

A visitor at Google searches for "vitamin A deficiency" and visits the first page in the SERPs. Not finding what they want, they click the back button on their browser to return to Google and repeat the search for "vitamin A deficiency".

What did that tell Google?

It told them that the visitor did not find the information they wanted on that page because they returned to Google and repeated (or refined) the search.

If lots of people around the world searched for a phrase, and an unusually high percentage bounced back from the same webpage ranked #1 in Google, what do you think Google would do?

Doesn't it make sense they would demote that page in the SERPs **for that particular search phrase,** since lots of people are not finding it relevant for that search query?

Bounce rates go hand-in-hand with relevance. If visitors find a page relevant for their search query, they'll stay on site. They might eventually bounce back to Google, but Google will know how long that visitor spent away from Google and can determine whether it is likely they found what they wanted.

5. Time a visitor stays on your page / site.

Google monitors the time visitors stay on web pages. One of the ways they do this is through their Google Analytics platform, which is free for webmasters to use. Because it is free, a lot of webmasters install it on their sites giving Google the ability to accurately track site visitors. It'll track time on site, the route a visitor takes through your site, how many pages they visit, what operating system, screen resolution, device they are using, and so on.

Most of the on-page factors are within the control of the webmaster. Even bounce rates and the time the visitor stays on your site is within your control to a certain extent. Provide the quality content and rich experience they are after, and you'll get lower bounce rates while keeping the visitor on your page/site for longer.

Off Page Factors

1. Click through rates (CTR)

This is something we should be paying particular attention to, and to a certain extent it is within our control. If you are not familiar with click through rates, let me give you an example.

Let's say a web page is ranked in position #5 on Google, and searchers seem to like that listing in the SERPs, with 15% of people clicking on it. Usually a page listed in position 5 would get around 5% of the clicks. Google will see more people than expected clicking that link, and give it a boost in the rankings. After all, it's apparently what the searchers are looking for.

On the other side of the coin, imagine a spammer (that's an "official" term used by Google to describe someone trying to manipulate rankings for a page) manages to bypass Google's algorithm with a "loophole", and ranks #1 for a search term. In position 1, a link typically gets 31% of the clicks, but this one only gets 15% because searchers are not impressed with the link title or description. On top of that, 95% of people who visit that link bounce right back to Google within 30 seconds of clicking the link. Google therefore has clear user signals that the web page ranking #1 is not popular with searchers and starts moving it down the rankings. This means that bad content will rarely get to the top of Google and stay there for any length of time.

2. Social signals

Social signals like Google +1s, Tweets, Facebook shares, Pinterest pins and so on, are clearly used as ranking factors in Google, though very minor ones. However, any boost they might offer will be short-lived because of the transient nature of social buzz.

For example, a new piece of content goes viral and is shared around by thousands of people via social media channels in a short space of time. Google will take notice of this, realize the content is something visitors want to see, and give it a ranking boost. After social interest peaks and shares start to decline, so will the ranking boost in Google.

Social sharing is great to encourage on your site, but don't expect the backlinks created from social channels to give you a big (or long-lasting) ranking boost.

3. Backlinks

When "webpage A" links to "webpage B" on another site, page B gets a "backlink", which Google sees as page A voting for page B. The general idea is that the more backlinks a page gets, the more "votes" it is getting from other sites on the web. The more votes, the more important it must be.

Today and for the foreseeable future, backlinks remain one of the most important rankings factors in Google's algorithm. However, more is not always better. Let me give you an example.

A web page that has **dozens** of links from authority sites like CNN, BBC, NYTimes etc is clearly an important web page. A page that has **thousands** of backlinks from low quality websites probably is not. Clearly backlinks can be a powerful indicator of a page's value, but just as clearly, not all backlinks are equal.

What Google needs to do is "grade" backlinks according to their worth. Backlinks from high quality "authority" web pages will count more than a backlink from a low quality page. Therefore, a page that gets a lot of high quality backlinks is likely to be able to rank well in Google. A page that has a lot of low quality backlinks will struggle to rank, and may even be penalized by Google for too many poor quality links!

Google's battle for survival

Over the years, Google has had to change and adapt to survive. It has been in constant battle with webmasters eager to manipulate the SERPs. Since the algorithm is based on real factors and properties of a website, webmasters have been trying to identify those factors and use them to their advantage. Whenever webmasters find a competitive advantage (sometimes called a loophole), Google tries to plug it.

For example, over a decade ago webmasters found out that Google used the Meta Keyword tag as a major ranking factor so began stuffing this tag with keywords in an attempt to rank well for those terms. Google started ignoring the Meta Keyword tag, effectively closing that loophole.

I would like to point out that I do believe Google still look at the Meta Keyword tag, but not as you might think. I believe Google use it to help identify spammers. Any page that has a Meta keyword tag stuffed with dozens (or hundreds) of keywords is clearly doing something underhand.

Here is another example of a loophole being closed.

A few years ago, webmasters found out that by using a domain name which essentially consisted of nothing more than the keyword phrase they wanted to rank for, the site would get a massive ranking boost in the SERPs. This type of domain is called an EMD and we'll look at them later. Anyway, in September 2012, Google released the "EMD Update" which removed that unfair ranking advantage. Hundreds of thousands of EMD sites dropped out of the Google top 10 overnight, and saw the end of a large industry in buying and selling EMDs.

Since an EMD is usually a commercial search phrase, most inbound links to these EMD sites also contained that exact commercial term. This over-optimization for a commercial phrase was bad news for the site owner, since Google's Penguin was on the lookout for this type of over-optimization.

Today, EMD sites are rarely seen in the top 10 for any mildly competitive search terms.

The battle between spammer and search engine continues to rage today. Spammers find loopholes, and Google plugs them. In September 2011, Google CEO Eric Schmidt said that Google had tested over 13,000 possible updated in 2010, approving 516 of them. 516 may sound a lot (it's more than one update a day), but it certainly wasn't an unusual year. Google probably update their algorithm at least 500-600 times every year. Most of these updates will be minor, but Google does roll out major changes every now and again. We'll look at the more important ones in the next chapter.

The one thing all Google updates have in common is that they are designed to improve the search results for the people that use the search engine – your potential visitors.

Panda, Penguin and other Major Updates

In February 2011, Google released the Panda update. The update was designed to filter out low quality web pages from the index. This was necessary because an earlier release (codenamed caffeine) massively increased the number of web pages that Google needed to handle - much of which was low quality. At the time, Panda left webmasters scratching their heads as to why their sites were penalized. The answer was simple – their pages were not deemed sufficient quality. Panda has since undergone a number of updates, most recently (at the time of writing this book) in September 2014 when Panda 4.1 was released. That was the 27th update to Panda.

On 24th April 2012, Google unleashed the Penguin which was initially called the "Webspam Update". If Panda was a 1 on the Richter scale of updates, Penguin was surely a 10. It completely changed the way we needed to think about SEO. Penguin's job was to find web pages that had been optimized above and beyond Google's "tolerance level", and punish them accordingly. That was a huge change and meant too much SEO was now a bad thing that could get a site penalized! With Penguin's arrival, just about everything we had learned about SEO in the previous 10 years had to be thrown out the Window. Google had moved the goal posts.

On 22nd May 2013, Google unleashed Penguin 2.0 which went far deeper than the original Penguin algorithm. This was not just a data refresh, but a major update to Penguin itself. An SEO's job just got a lot harder, and it would only get tougher.

On June 11th 2013, Google released the "Payday Loan" update which targeted niches with notoriously spammy SERPs. These niches were often highly commercial, offering great rewards for any page that could rank highly, so they were targeted by spammers. Google gave the example of "payday loans" when announcing this update, hence its name. This is another major anti-spam update which has seen further updates in Payday Loans 2.0 and Payday Loans 3.0 in 2014.

On 26th September 2013 Google announced another major update, called Hummingbird. This update had actually rolled out around the 20th August 2013, but was less likely to have caused you problems than Panda or Penguin. Rather than just an update to the existing algorithm, Hummingbird was a completely new algorithm. Think of the algorithm as the code that sorts through all of the available information to find the best results for any query. Hummingbird was a new and modern engine installed in Google. We'll look at it in a moment.

In July 2014, Google unleashed the Pigeon update. This one was related to local search results. We also saw Penguin 3.0 on 17th October 2014, and then the Pirate 2.0 update a few days later on the 21st October. The original pirate update was in August 2012, and was previously called the DMCA penalty. As the name suggests, the Pirate update was released to help combat software and digital media piracy.

Hummingbird – fast & accurate?

Hummingbird is the name given to Google's latest search algorithm. That's not a part of the algorithm, or a minor algorithm update, but the entire brand-spanking new algorithm that was unboxed and moved into place on August 20th 2013.

This is a major change to the way Google sorts through the information in its index and a change of this scale has probably not occurred for over a decade.

Think of it this way. Panda and Penguin were changes to parts of the old algorithm, whereas Hummingbird is a completely new algorithm, although it still uses components of the old one.

The algorithm is basically the mathematical equation(s) used to determine the most relevant pages to return in the search results. The equation is built of over 200 components, things like PageRank and incoming links, etc.

Apparently the name Hummingbird was chosen because of how fast and accurate these birds are. Although a lot of webmasters would disagree, Google obviously thinks this reflects their search results.

Google wanted to introduce a major update to the algorithm because of the evolution in the way people use Google to search. An example Google has given is in "conversation search" where people can now speak into their mobile phone, tablet or even desktop browser to find information. Imagine you were interested in buying a Nexus 7 tablet. The old way of finding it online was to type something like this in the Google search box:

Buy Nexus 7

However, with speech, people have become a lot more descriptive in what they are searching for. For example, it's easy to just dictate into your search browser something like:

"Where can I buy a Nexus 7 near here?"

The old Google could not cope too well with this search phrase, but the new Hummingbird is designed to do just that. The old Google would look for pages in the index that included some or all of the words in the search phrase. A page that included the exact phrase would have the best chance of appearing at the top of Google. If no pages were found with the exact phrase, then Google would look for pages that included the important words from that phrase, e.g. "where" "buy" and "nexus 7".

The idea behind Hummingbird is that it should be able to interpret what the searcher is really looking for. In this case, they are clearly looking for somewhere near their current location where they can purchase a Nexus 7.

In other words, Hummingbird is suppose to determine searcher intent and return pages that best match that intent (as opposed to best matching keywords in the search phrase). Hummingbird tries to understand exactly what the searcher wants, rather than just taking into account the words used in the search term.

Today, optimizing for specific keyword phrases has not just become difficult (because of Panda & Penguin), it has become less effective in driving traffic if those phrases do not match the intent of the searcher typing those phrases into Google.

Out of all of these updates, the one that had the biggest influence on my own SEO was Penguin. Google sent their Penguin into places that no SEO professional ever imagined Google would dare. April 24th 2012 was the day the world of SEO changed forever. It was also the day that inspired me to release the first edition of this book entitled **"SEO 2012 & Beyond – SEO will never be the same again"**. Google created such a major shift in the way it analyzed pages that I now think in terms of Pre-Penguin and Post-Penguin SEO, and that will likely come across in this book.

SEO Today

Today, SEO is very different from even a couple of years ago. Google has put a number of measures in place to combat the manipulative actions of webmasters.

Ask a bunch of webmasters to define the term SEO and I bet you'll get a lot of different answers. Definitions will differ depending on the type of person you ask and even when you ask them. SEO before Google introduced the Panda update was easy. After the Panda update it was still relatively easy, but you needed to make sure your content was good. After Google released the Penguin update, SEO suddenly became a whole lot harder.

In 2015, phrases you'll hear being used by SEOs include:

- On-page SEO
- Off-page SEO
- Link building
- Black hat SEO
- Grey hat SEO
- White hat SEO

We've looked briefly at the first three of those, so let me quickly define the last three with a diagram.

Types of SEO Techniques

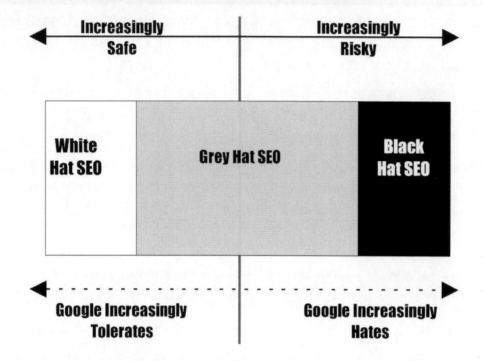

In the diagram above, we have three forms of SEO:

1. **White Hat SEO** – approved strategies for getting your page to rank well. Google offers guidelines to webmasters which spell out approved SEO strategies.
2. **Black Hat SEO** – these are the "loopholes" that Google are actively seeking out and penalizing for. They include a whole range of strategies from on-page keyword stuffing to backlink blasts using software to generate tens of thousands of backlinks to a webpage.
3. **Grey Hat SEO** – Strategies that lie between the two extremes. These are strategies that Google do not approve of, but are less likely to get your site penalized than black hat SEO. They are certainly riskier than white hat SEO, but not as risky as black hat.

If you think of this as a sliding scale from totally safe "White Hat" SEO to totally dangerous "Black Hat" SEO, then you can imagine that as you move to the right with your SEO, you are more likely to get into hot water with Google (at least in the long term). As you move more to the left with your SEO, you are more likely to be safer with Google. Google's tolerance level is somewhere in the grey hat area.

Staying in the middle may give you better returns for your time, but you risk a penalty eventually.

Before Panda & Penguin, most webmasters knew where these lines were drawn and took their risks accordingly.

When Google introduced Panda, the only real change to this was that webmasters needed to make sure that their website content was unique, interesting to visitors, AND added something that maybe no other webpage on the topic had. No small task, but to beat Panda, the goal was to create excellent content.

When Google introduced Penguin, they completely changed the face of SEO, probably forever, or at least as long as Google continues to be the dominant search engine (which probably amounts to the same thing). Here is a diagrammatic representation of how SEO changed:

Post Penguin & Panda

Increasingly Risky

| White Hat SEO | Grey Hat SEO | Black Hat SEO |

Google Approved Strategies

Increasing chance of a penalty

Google Tolerance

We've still got White Hat and Black Hat, but grey hat has become a lot riskier.

The "increasingly risky, increasingly safe" vertical divider that I drew in the centre of the first diagram (pre-Panda & Penguin) has now moved to the left and is right up against the edge of the white hat SEO.

You'll notice that there is a new "Google Tolerance" line drawn on the diagram. This tolerance line can move left to right, depending on how Google tweak their algorithm. If they want to come down hard on "spammers", they'll move the line to the left. If too many good sites get taken out as "collateral damage", they may move the tolerance line to the right a bit (although see the section later on "Trust v No-Trust"). Generally though, for all new sites and most others, the tolerance level is very close to the White hat boundary.

A webmaster that uses techniques which are further to the right than this tolerance line is risking their rankings.

Although these diagrams are good to work from, they do not display the whole truth.

Let's just consider how trust changes the equation.

Trust Vs no-trust

The Google Tolerance line will slide left or right depending on the site that is being ranked. For a site that has proven its worth and Google trusts a lot, we might see the diagram like this:

A trusted site

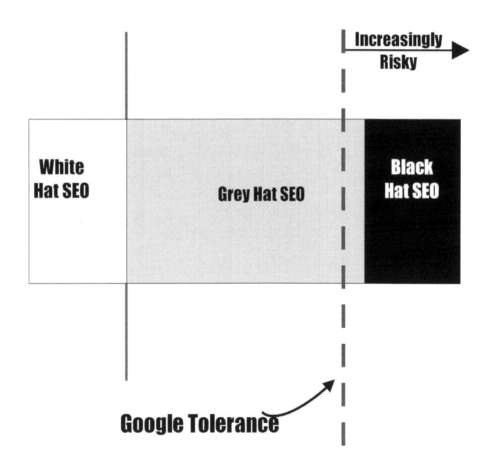

Yet for a new site, or one that has no track record to speak of, the diagram will probably look a lot more like this.

A non-trusted site

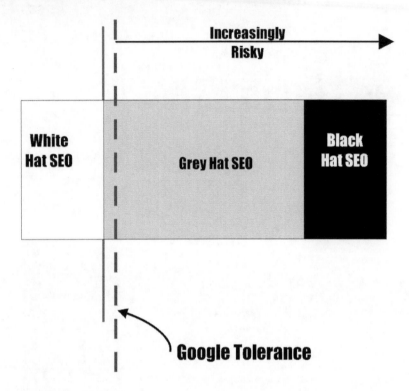

The only difference is in the location of the dashed "tolerance line".

In other words, Google are a lot more tolerant to sites that have built up authority and trust than they are to new sites, or sites that have not been able to attain a decent level of authority.

A high authority site with lots of trust can withstand a certain amount of spammy SEO without incurring a penalty (see later when we discuss "negative SEO"). The more authority, the more it can endure.

A new site on the other hand, would be quickly penalized for even a small amount of spammy SEO.

Webmasters living in the past

A lot of webmasters (or SEO companies vying for your business) may disagree with my take on modern-day SEO, and that's fine. The more people who just don't get it, the less competition there is for me and my clients.

I am sure you can find people that will say this is all rubbish and that they can get your pages ranked for your search terms (depending on the severity of competition of course), by heavily backlinking the page using keyword rich anchor text.

The process they'll describe is eerily similar to the process I told you about in the section "How we used to rank pages" earlier (i.e. before 2010). It goes something like this:

1. Keyword research to find high demand, low competition phrases.
2. Create a page that is optimized for that keyword phrase.
3. Get lots of backlinks using that keyword phrase as anchor text.
4. Watch your page rise up the SERPs.

If you don't care about your business, then follow that strategy or hire someone to do it for you. You might get short term gains, but you'll run the risk of losing all your rankings further down the line when Google catches up with you (and catch up it will... eventually).

To lose all of your rankings does not take a human review, though Google does use human reviewers on some occasions. No, getting your site penalized is far easier and the process Google has created is far more "automated" since the introduction of Panda and Penguin. Go over the threshold levels of what is acceptable, and the penalty is algorithmically determined and applied.

The good news is that algorithmic penalties can just as easily be lifted by removing the offending SEO and cleaning up your site. However, if that offending SEO includes low quality backlinks to your site (especially to the homepage), things are a little trickier.

Remember the SEO expert you hired that threw tens of thousands of backlinks at your site using his secret software? How can you get those backlinks removed? In many cases you can't but Google do provide a "Disavow" tool that can help in many instances. I'll tell you about that later in the book. In extreme circumstances, moving the site to a new domain may be your only option.

In the rest of this book, I want to focus on what you need to do to help your pages rank better. I'll be focusing mainly on white-hat strategies, though I will venture into grey hat SEO as well. I won't be covering black-hat SEO at all because it is just not a long-term strategy. Remember, with the flick of a switch Google can move the goal posts again, leaving you out in the cold. Is it worth risking your business for short-term gains?

Let's get started with the 4 pillars of post-Penguin SEO.

The 4 pillars of post-Penguin SEO

I have been doing SEO for over 10 years now and I have always concentrated on long-term strategies. That's not to say I haven't dabbled in black hat SEO. Over the years, I have done a lot of experiments on ranking factors. However without exception, all of the sites I promoted with black hat SEO have been penalized.

In this book, I don't want to talk about the murkier SEO strategies that will eventually cause you problems, so I'll concentrate on white hat, safe techniques.

I divide SEO into the four main pillars. These are:

1. Quality content
2. Site organization
3. Authority
4. What's in it for the visitor?

These are the four areas where you need to concentrate your efforts. So let's now have a look at each of them in turn.

1. Quality content

Before we begin, let me just say that a lot of SEO "experts" have disagreed with me on the need for quality content as a major ranking factor. They will often cite exceptions in the search engines where pages rank well for competitive terms without any on-page content. The fact that these exceptions rarely last more than a week or two escapes them. Remember, bounce rates and time on site are indicators to Google of whether a page gives a visitor what they want. Poor content cannot hide in the Google top 10. It essentially gets voted out by the search engine users who vote with the length of time they stay on a site, and what they do when they return to Google.

If you are one of those people that questions the need for quality content, then I encourage you to watch a video I recorded before you read the rest of this book. You can watch the video here:

http://ezseonews.com/lsivid

It's quite an eye opener.

What Google Tell us about quality content

Google's Webmaster Guidelines offer advice to webmasters. They tell us what Google considers good content, and what they consider spam. Let's take a quick look at what the guidelines say about content.

1. Create a useful, information-rich site

This one should be obvious. Create content that your visitors want to see.

2. Think about the words people use to search

.. and try to incorporate them into your pages. This particular guideline is one that I think will soon disappear, as it is an invitation to webmasters to fill their pages with keywords and phrases. Focusing on keywords usually results in a web page that is optimized for the search engines at the expense of the visitor's experience, and Google openly label that type of page as Webspam.

I think this guideline is probably left over from the pre-Panda days, and better advice (which you'll understand if you watched that video earlier in this chapter), is to think about the words people use to search, synonyms of those words and the searchers intent. What is the searcher looking for exactly? What words, phrases and topics does your page need to satisfy that intent? We will look at this in more detail later.

3. Try to use text instead of images for important names, content or links

Google's crawler does not recognize text in images, so if there is an important word or phrase that you need Google to know exists in an important part of your site, use text. If it has to be an image for whatever reason, then use the ALT tag of the image to create a description of the image that includes that phrase.

A great example of using text instead of images is in links on your site. Links are the most important factor in SEO, so the more the search engines know about the nature of a link the better. If you are linking to a page on your site about "purple furbies", then use **purple furbies** as the link text. This will tell Google that you (the webmaster) think the page you are linking to is about purple furbies. These internal links also help rank a page for a specific term. Internal links are a safer way to get keyword rich anchor text into a link (something that is not safe coming from other websites). See the section on backlinking later.

4. Make <title> and ALT attributes descriptive

The <title> tag of your page is one of the most important areas in terms of SEO. Try to get your most important keyword in there, but don't stuff keywords. The title has two main objectives; enticing the searcher to click through from the search engines, and to tell Google what your page is about.

We talked about click through rates (CTR) earlier in the book and how important a factor they are in modern SEO. If you find that a page has a low CTR (you can check in Google webmaster tools), tweak the title to see if you can make it more enticing to searchers, and monitor the CTR of the page. Better titles (that match the searcher's intent) will attract more clicks in the Google SERPs.

NOTE: When a page is listed in the search results, it also contains a description. This is often taken from the Meta Description tag of your page, but not always. You can do the same tweaking of the Meta description tag to increase CTR, but it's less of an exact science since Google will sometimes grab text from elsewhere on the page for the listing's description.

ALT tags are there for a purpose. They are there to help people that have images turned off, for example people with impaired vision. Often they'll use text to voice software to read pages, so your ALT tags should help them. It should describe the image to those users in a concise way. It is also a great place to insert a keyword phrase or synonym, but never use ALT tags simply as a place to insert keywords.

5. Make pages for users, not search engines

This is probably the most important point in all of the Webmaster guidelines. If you keep this in mind at all times, you'll be on the right path.

Don't just create content for search engines in the hope of ranking better and building more traffic. Create the content that your audience wants to see. By keeping your visitors happy, Google are happy, and your authority and traffic will build in a safe way.

6. Avoid tricks designed to manipulate your rankings

Google offer you a rule of thumb. If you are comfortable explaining what you are doing to a Google employee, or one of your competitors (who could report you to Google), then you are probably doing things properly. Another great test is to ask yourself whether or not you would do what you are doing if search engines did not exist.

7. Make your website stand out in your field

No matter what niche you are in, no matter what keywords you want to rank for, you ultimately have 10 other pages competing with you. They are the 10 pages at the top of the SERPs. That's where you want to rank, isn't it? Therefore ignore all of the other thousands of pages ranking page 2 and beyond, and concentrate on the top 10 pages. How can you make your page stand out from these competitors? How can you make your page better, more engaging, different and valuable? Google need to see that your page adds to the top 10 in a unique way, not blend in with them.

Google tells us to avoid the following

1. Automatically generated content.

In an effort to build websites faster, webmasters have created a variety of tools, including some that can create content for you. Obviously the content is very poor quality and considered spam by Google. Any tool or service that offers to generate content for you should be avoided at all costs. This will get your site penalized or even de-indexed (removed from Google).

Some webmasters go so far as to have pages automatically generated (and updated) out of stuff on other websites. For example, they can use various data feeds (these are databases that contain information like product listings, articles, etc) and RSS feeds to populate pages that have no unique or original content. As the feeds are updated, so are the pages on the site. The only time using datafeeds is a good idea is if you own the feed and its contents will be unique to your own site (e.g. an e-commerce site using a product feed).

2. Creating pages with little or no original content.

Commonly called thin page, these are pages that don't really offer much value to the visitor. They include pages with very little content, or pages that might have a lot of content but it's not original. Being original is more than just having a unique article that passes Copyscape. Being original means offering new ideas, thoughts and insights that are not found in other pages in the top 10.

3. Hidden text.

In an effort to rank for more terms, some webmasters have tried making some text on the page invisible. This typically includes keyword rich text using lots of related terms the webmaster wishes to rank for. This used to work several years ago, but today it will get your site penalized.

Hidden links also come under the umbrella of hidden text. This has been used in the past to spread link juice around, maybe by linking a full stop (period) to another page in an effort to make it rank better.

There are a number of ways of hiding to hide text on a pages, but Google are on to all of them, so don't do it.

4. Doorway pages.

This term refers to pages that are set up to rank for a single specific keyword phrase. They are highly optimized for that phrase, and their sole purpose is to rank high for that phrase. Traffic is then typically (though not always) funnelled to another page or site.

5. Scraped content.

This is content that has been copied from other web sites. Spammers often do this to add more content to their own website quickly.

Scraping can be entire articles, or just part of another webpage. Scraping includes copying someone else's content and swapping out synonyms in an attempt to make it unique.

Even pages that embed videos or other media (e.g. Youtube videos) into their pages will be considered scraped content unless the webmaster adds their own unique commentary or thoughts to the page. A webpage should offer value to a visitor, even if all scraped content is removed.

6. Participating in affiliate programs without adding sufficient value.

One of Google's recent algorithm changes targeted web pages that were heavy on adverts. Google reasons that too many ads on a page make for a bad user experience. Therefore adverts should be seen as secondary to the main content.

Another thing to be aware of is that if you run a review site, your reviews need to be unique and contain original thoughts and ideas. Your reviews need to contain information that is not available on the merchant site, or other affiliate sites.

If you simply go to Amazon and use their product description and user comments, then your page is not only scraped content, it's also fails to add sufficient value. Reviews need to have original thoughts, ideas and suggestions to be of any value. Why would someone want to read your review when they can read all of the same information on Amazon or the manufacturer's site?

A good test is to strip out all of the adverts and content that was scraped (even if you re-wrote it in your own words) from a page and see whether the page still offers sufficient value to the visitor.

7. Loading pages with keywords.

In an effort to rank for more terms, some webmasters stuff keywords into their page. Quite often you'll see a list of keywords on the page, maybe a "related terms" section, or a list of US states.

Another way pages can be loaded with keywords is by re-using keywords or phrases too many times so that the sentence is unnatural or grammatically incorrect.

Google offer this example:

"We sell **custom cigar humidors**. Our **custom cigar humidors** are handmade. If you're thinking of buying a **custom cigar humidor**, please contact our **custom cigar humidor** specialists at **custom.cigar.humidors**@example.com."

See how that is totally unnatural?

Loading pages with keywords is clearly something that is only done for the benefit of the search engines, so will be penalized.

8. User-generated spam.

A good example of user-generated spam is comments on your site. If you accept comments, and you should, they must be moderated. In addition, only accept legitimate comments that add to the "conversation" you started on the page. Never approve comments that simply attempt to stroke your ego (like "great blog"), or ask irrelevant questions (like "what Wordpress theme is this?"). Only approve comments that raise legitimate points, or ask legitimate questions about your article.

Another type of user-generated content you need to be careful about is guest posts. If you accept articles from other people and post them on your site, you must never accept any content that is below your own standards. I would also recommend you never allow external links in the body of the article. If the author wants to include a link back to their website, only allow it in the author bio section at the end of the article, and make these links nofollow. When I have suggested this in the past, people have complained that if they follow my guidelines they won't get people to write guest posts because there is nothing in it for the writer. My reply is that if they don't follow these guidelines, they won't have a site to accept guest posts on. If your site reaches authority status in your niche, then writers will benefit from the exposure they would not otherwise receive, and the status of their backlink is a lot less important.

A summary quality content & an example

There are a number of different types of content that you can add to your site including articles, product reviews, quizzes, videos etc. However, no matter what type of content you are looking at, it has to:

1. Be created for the visitor, not the search engines. That means it needs to read well and have no visible signs of keyword stuffing.
2. Add value to the top 10 SERPs (if you want to rank in the top 10, your page has to be seen as adding something unique to that collection of pages).
3. Give your visitors what they want. Create the content they want to see.

To put it simply, all of the content on your site has to be the best you can make it.

A good rule of thumb suggested by Google is this; would your content look out of place if it were published in a glossy magazine?

If you hire ghostwriters, proof read their content to make sure that any **facts are correct** and there are **no spelling or grammatical errors.**

As you read through the content that you intend to post onto your website, ask yourself:

• Is it content that your visitors will find useful?

• Is there information in there that your visitors are unlikely to know, and therefore find informative?

• If it's a review, does it sound overly hyped up? Are both sides of the argument covered (i.e. positives and negatives)? Is there information in the review that is not available on the manufacturer's website or other affiliate sites? Does the review offer a different way of looking at things which may help the buyer make a better informed decision prior to purchase?

So we know that Google wants. Let's take a look at some poor content.

Here is the first paragraph of an article I found online a few years ago. Can you guess what **the** author was trying to optimize the page for?

Understanding Pomegranate Juice Benefits

Some people may not be that knowledgeable about pomegranate juice benefits but it is actually a very effective source of Vitamin C. The pomegranate fruit contains a lot of healthy nutrients and you can get a lot of good immune system boosters out of pomegranate juice benefits. It can actually provide around 16% of the required amount of Vitamin C that adults need to take on a daily basis. Pomegranate juice benefits also include Vitamin B5 as well as the antioxidant element of polyphenols and potassium.

This page is no longer found in Google. I wonder why? ;)

The underlined keywords are part of the Kontera advertising system, so just ignore that.

It's not too difficult to guess the main phrase the author was targeting, is it? In fact, it reminds me of the Google "do not do" example we saw earlier about custom cigar humidors.

"Pomegranate juice benefits" sticks out like a sore thumb. In fact, in a relatively short article (415 words) that phrase appeared 17 times. That's a density of 4%!

How many people think a density of 4% is OK or natural? Is repeating the same phrase 4 times every 100 words natural? Do you want to know what a natural density is?

Let me tell you... Are you ready?

Natural density of a keyword phrase is **whatever density occurs naturally when an expert in their field writes an article**.

If you look back at that pomegranate paragraph, there is an even bigger sin.

This sentence does not make sense:

"The pomegranate fruit contains a lot of healthy nutrients and you can get a lot of good immune system boosters out of **pomegranate juice benefits.**"

It doesn't make sense, does it? It should finish with "..out of pomegranate juice", but the webmasters used it as an opportunity to stuff in that main phrase again, making the sentence nonsense.

This is a very clear indicator that the author was stuffing that phrase into the article in an attempt to help the article rank higher for that phrase.

The sad thing is that this type of article may well have ranked well before Panda and Penguin. Why is that sad? Because web searchers had to put up with this kind of rubbish.

Today, no amount of sneaky black hat techniques could get this page into the top 10 (at least not for the long term). That is the difference between pre and post Panda/Penguin SEO. It's the reason this page no longer exists in Google, or in fact online. The webmaster has closed the site down, presumably after it stopped being profitable.

If I do a Google search for **pomegranate juice benefits**, the top ranked page (at the time of writing) does NOT include the exact phrase at all! How's that for a natural density? The number 2 ranked site includes it once in 2696 words (a density of 0.04%), and the #3 ranked page does not include the term at all.

The lesson to learn from this is to throw keyword density rules out of the window.

What may be a surprise to many, is that out of the top 10 pages ranking for the term "pomegranate juice benefits", only ONE has that phrase in the page title. In fact, **only one** (the same one) of the top 10 pages includes that phrase anywhere in the article.

Perhaps you think that statistic is just a fluke?

Try it with any search term that isn't a brand name or product name. In general, the top 10 search results in Google list far fewer pages containing the actual search term, and this number has decreased over the last year (since I last updated this book).

So just how is Google able to decide how to rank webpages for the term "pomegranate juice benefits" (or any other search term), if they are not looking for that actual phrase in the content?

The answer to that does lie with the words on the page, but in a less obvious, though totally natural way.

Let me ask you a question.

Does your article sound as if it was written by an expert?

The reason I ask is because when an article is written by somebody who really knows their subject, they will use a certain "niche vocabulary". That is, they will use words and phrases that actually define the topic of the article.

You can read an article I wrote over three years ago called "Niche Vocabulary - why poor content can't hide in Google".

http://famousbloggers.net/niche-vocabulary-poor-content-google.html

You will see in that article, that if your content does not contain its niche vocabulary, you're very unlikely to rank well in Google.

Every article you write will have its own niche vocabulary.

Articles on related topics may well use a lot of the same niche vocabulary, but they will also contain other words and phrases that define the topic more specifically.

Let's look at an example.

To carry out a test, I found a number of words on the top 10 pages of Google ranking for the term epilepsy. These words appeared on many of the top 10 pages ranking for that term. These are what I call theme words (or niche vocabulary), i.e. words that commonly appear in articles that are written on a given topic.

Here are the theme words I found for the term epilepsy:

age, aid, anti, brain, cause, children, control, develop, diagnosis, diet, doctor, drugs, epilepsy, epileptic, guide, health, help, home, information, ketogenic, life, living, log, medical, medications, part, plan, research, seizure, seizure-free, seizures, side, special, support, surgery, symptoms, take, term, test, time, treatment, types, unit, work

I then chose two sub-niches in the epilepsy fields to see if these words appeared on those pages as well. The sub niches were:

1. Epilepsy treatment
2. Ketogenic diet

Both of these terms are highly related to epilepsy (the ketogenic diet is a diet that helps cure epilepsy in a number of patients). Since they are both talking about epilepsy, they both should contain a lot of the epilepsy niche vocabulary.

First let's have a look at the top ranking pages for the term **epilepsy**. Here is a screenshot showing the number one ranked article with the theme words I found earlier highlighted in the text:

isturbed **brain** activity that **cause** changes in attention or behavior. se
ses, incidence, and risk factors **epilepsy** occurs when permanent cha
te **cause** the **brain** to be too excitable or jumpy. the **brain** sends out
als. this results in repeated, unpredictable **seizures**. (a single **seizure**
pen again is not **epilepsy**.) **epilepsy** may be due to a **medical** condit
affects the **brain**, or the **cause** may be unknown (idiopathic). comm
epsy include: stroke or transient ischemic attack (tia) dementia, such
ase traumatic **brain** injury infections, including **brain** abscess, mening
aids **brain** problems that are present at birth (congenital **brain** defec
occurs during or near bith metabolism disorders that a child may be b
henylketonuria) **brain** tumor abnormal blood vessels in the **brain** oth
tage or destroy **brain** tissue **epilepsy seizures** usually begin betwee
but they can happen at any **age**. there may be a family history of **seiz**
epsy. **symptoms symptoms** vary from person to person. some peop
ole staring spells, while others have violent shaking and loss of alertnes
ure depends on the **part** ██████ **brain** affected and **cause** of **epileps**
a. the **seizure** is similar to the previous one. some people with **epilep**

You can only see a small section of the article here, as it's quite long, but I'm sure you'll agree that the theme words are well sprinkled throughout.

Let's repeat this but using the number one ranked article for the term **epilepsy treatment**:

with the introduction of **dilantin** (warner-lambert), has been a triumph of mode
te. the **development** of newer **medications**, **especially** tegretol (ciba-geigy) an
(reckitt & colman) has meant that **epilepsy** can be suppressed in most patients
t serious or annoying **side** effects. this is not to say that every patient can be fully
lled, or that **side** effects do not occur. a continuing effort is being made by
tional pharmaceutical companies to find safer, more effective **treatment**██████
sy. new **drugs** are not cascading onto the market however, for the high cost of
ch, development and marketing (about a$150 million for any new drug) is an
nt disincentive. how do **drugs** prevent **seizures**? strange to say, most of the
used in treating **epilepsy** today were discovered to have **anti-epileptic** propert
nce. we have used these **drugs** with great benefit for years without really knowi
ey **work**. however, a more systematic search for new **anti**epileptic██████s is n
vay, based on **research** progress in understanding how neurones transmit
:s to each other, and our increasing knowledge of the structure and function of t
ane which surrounds each neurone. the messages that one neurone sends to the
leditated by releasing neurotransmitter chemicals, can either excite the neurone
line, or can inhibit its electrical activity. the identification of gamaa-amino butyric

Once again we see the theme words sprinkled throughout the content as we would expect, since this article is also about epilepsy.

Let's now look at the final example, which is the **ketogenic diet**:

ketogenic diet was then gradually forgotten as new **anticonvulsant** **medications** developed. the **ketogenic diet** has recently been 'rediscovered' and is achieving increasingly widespread use. its modern day role as alternative management for cl with difficult-to-**control epilepsy** is currently being re-defined. the **ketogenic die** a 'fad' or a 'quack **diet**', but rather is an alternative **medical treatment** childr difficult-to-**control epilepsy**. the **ketogenic diet** should only be used under the supervision of a physician and a **dietician**. background fasting to achieve **control** **seizure** was described in both the bible and during the middle **ages**, but it was o during the early 1920s that scientific papers first appeared describing the beneficia effects of prolonged fasting for **children** whose **epilepsy** could not be **controlled** few **medications** then available. these papers claimed that starvation, drinking onl for 10 to 20 or more days, could result in **control seizure** for prolonged peri **time**. during this era, when the metabolic effects of diabetes were also being studi was noted that the biochemical effects of fasting could be mimicked by eating a di

This too has the theme words for epilepsy sprinkled throughout.

Since all of these articles have epilepsy theme words sprinkled throughout them, they could all theoretically rank for the term epilepsy. Google will know these articles are about epilepsy because they contain epilepsy-related words and phrases.

In addition to the core set of epilepsy-related theme words, each of these articles also contain **a slightly different set of theme words** which help to define what area of epilepsy they are discussing. We could show this by finding theme words specific to each of the three articles. We would see words and phrases with a different emphasis popping up (though there would be a core of epilepsy related words).

To show this, I found a number of "theme phrases" – 2, 3 & 4 word phrases that are common to the top 10 ranked pages for the three terms – epilepsy, epilepsy treatment & ketogenic diet.

Here is a table of the results, showing the theme words and phrases appearing in the top 10 pages ranked for each of the search terms:

Epilepsy	Epilepsy Treatment	Ketogenic Diet
activity in the brain	adverse effects	anticonvulsant drug
atkins diet	aid for seizures	anticonvulsant drugs
blood sugar	anticonvulsant drug	beta hydroxybutyric acid
causes of epilepsy	anticonvulsant drugs	body fat
epilepsy medication	anti-epileptic drug	control of seizures
epilepsy medications	anti-epileptic	control seizures
epilepsy surgery	medications	diet controls seizures
ketogenic diet	anti-seizure	different anticonvulsants
part of the brain	medications	high fat
seizure medicines	controlling seizures	high fat diet
temporal lobe	epileptic control	high fat intake
vagus nerve	epileptic seizures	medical treatment for children
	ketogenic diet	protein and carbohydrate
	seizure control	seizure control
	seizure medications	seizure type
	temporal lobe	treatment of seizure
	treatment of epilepsy	while on the diet
	treatments for	
	epilepsy	

This table clearly shows that each of the three search terms have a different niche vocabulary.

All three articles have theme words relating to epilepsy as we would expect. However each of the articles also had their own set of theme phrases which help to distinguish the actual sub-niche within epilepsy.

- The **epilepsy** article has a wide range of theme phrases relating to all aspects of epilepsy.
- The **epilepsy treatment** article focused more on phrases that are related to the treatment of epilepsy (big surprise eh?).
- The **ketogenic diet** article had more theme phrases relating to the diet itself and the control seizures.

Another Example?

Anyone that read earlier versions of this book will recognise the Epilepsy example from those earlier editions. Therefore, the example is a few years old and you may question whether or not the information is still valid today. Therefore, let's do a brand new example to see.

I ran an analysis of the top 10 pages ranking for the term "Health benefits of Krill Oil". By the way, not one page listed in the top 10 for that term (at the time of writing) had that exact phrase in the title!

Here are the theme words I found on 7 or more of the top 10 page:

acids, age, animal, balance, benefits, better, blood, capsules, cardiovascular, care, cell, cholesterol, clinical, daily, dha, diet, disease, eat, effects, epa, fatty, fish, flu, food, health, healthy, heart, human, krill, levels, liver, lower, nutrition, oil, omega-3, protein, ratio, red, reduce, research, safe, side, skin, source, sources, studies, study, supplement, supplements, test, women

There are 51 words in that list, and all 51 were found on 7 or more of the top 10 pages that rank for the term "health benefits of krill oil".

I also checked for 2, 3 and 4 word phrases that were found on the same top 10 page, and these are the ones I found:

allergic reaction, amino acid, bad cholesterol, benefits of krill, benefits of krill oil, brain health, cardiovascular disease, cell membranes, cholesterol levels, clinical studies, clinical study, cod liver, crp levels, daily dose, dietary supplement, effects of krill oil, experimental animal, eye health, fatty acids, fish oil, fish oil supplement, fish oil supplements, fish oils, food source, free radicals, health benefits, health care, health food, healthy cholesterol, heart disease, heart health, krill oil, krill oil arthritis benefits, krill oil benefit, krill oil daily, krill protein, lose weight, metabolic syndrome, nitric oxide, oil supplement, omega 3, omega-3 fatty acids, omega-3 phospholipid, omega-3 polyunsaturated fatty acids, pain killer, polyunsaturated fatty acids, premenstrual syndrome, rheumatoid arthritis, side effects, source of omega-3, sources of omega-3, triglyceride levels, weight loss

The difference between theme words and theme phrases in my analysis

The difference between theme words and theme phrases is obvious.

Theme words contain 1 word.

Theme phrases contain more than 1 word.

When it comes to Google, finding theme phrases in an article is further confirmation of a theme, but when I am analyzing top ranking pages, I concentrate on the theme words, not the phrases. Why? Well because theme phrases often have several variations which essentially mean the same thing, and ARE the same thing to Google. An example in the list above would include:

- fish oil supplement
- fish oil supplements

Both mean the same thing, and just because an article contains one instead of the other does not make one more important than the other.

A much better strategy would be to place the importance on the words that make up those phrases (fish, oil & supplement).

Here is another example:

- omega 3
- omega-3 fatty acids
- omega-3 phospholipid
- omega-3 polyunsaturated fatty acids

Just because an article on krill oil does not specifically use the phrase **omega-3 polyunsaturated fatty acids,** does not mean it hasn't talked about omega-3.

If I concentrate on the words **omega-3, fatty, acids, phospholipid and polyunsaturated** in my analysis, I can cover all variations of these phrases.

I hope you can see that there is not much point counting individual theme phrases. The *important theme phrases will be made up of the important theme words*, so that is what I concentrate on.

Back to the experiment…

I wanted to see how many of my 51 theme words were being used by pages ranked in the top 100 of Google.

For this analysis I grouped pages ranking in the following positions:

1-10, 11-20, 21-30, 31-40, 41-50 & 51-60

I wanted to see how well the pages in these positions were themed for my 51 keywords. I analysed each page individually, and then averaged out for the group.

Here are the results:

Position 1-10 on average used 86% of my theme words.

Position 11-20 on average used 81% of my theme words.

Position 21-30 on average used 78% of my theme words.

Position 31-40 on average used 69% of my theme words.

Position 41-50 on average used 69% of my theme words.

Position 51-60 on average used 73% of my theme words.

So, all of the pages in the top 60 contained a good number of my theme words, with a pages averaging between 69% - 86%.

Taking this a step further, I wanted to see how well those pages ranked further down the SERPs were themed.

I grabbed the URLs ranking at:

100-109, 200-209 and 300-309

Position 100-109 on average used 65% of my theme words.

Position 200-209 on average used 72% of my theme words.

Position 300-309 on average used 62% of my theme words.

That's right, even those web pages ranked down in the 100 – 300 range are well themed, containing a good proportion of my 51 theme words.

By the way, the reason I didn't analyse pages ranked lower than 300 is because Google doesn't actually include more than a few hundred URLs in their SERPs. Here, check this out:

Colon Cleanse Capsules, Eye Supplements, Krill Oil and Acai Capsules.

In order to show you the most relevant results, we have omitted some entries very similar to the 381 already displayed.
If you like, you can repeat the search with the omitted results included.

Searches related to health benefits of krill oil

health benefits of krill oil **to the skin**	health benefits **flax seed** oil
health benefits of krill oil **supplements**	krill oil **supplements**
health benefits **yerba mate tea**	benefits of krill oil **pills**
health benefits **fish** oil	**mega red** krill oil benefits

‹ Goooogle

Previous   1 2 3 **4**

I did a Google search for **health benefits of krill oil**, showing 100 results per page. On page 4, the results end with Google telling me that the rest of the pages in the index are similar to these 381! Therefore Google only ranks 381 pages for this phrase!

...ting that all of the pages included in the SERPs seem well themed around ...eme words, and we can harvest those theme words by analysing the top ...ogle for any given term.

my experiment

It's looking like all web pages ranked in Google for a search term are themed around a core set of keywords and phrases. Any page that does not cut the mustard doesn't appear in the main set of search results (the 381 pages we saw in the previous screen shot).

However, I had an idea to test this further. If all web pages really are themed around a group of related words, then I should be able to analyze the pages ranked 300-310 and grab the theme words from those pages, instead of the top 10. If I re-analyse the pages ranked in positions 1-10, 100-110, 200-210 & 300-310, I should find a similar high percentage of those theme words used in each case.

That is exactly what I did.

I extracted the theme words from the pages ranked 300-310 using Web Content Studio, and then refined the selection, only accepting theme words that appeared on 7 or more of those 10 pages. I ended up with a list of 49 theme words. Here they are:

acid, acids, antarctic, anti-inflammatory, antioxidant, antioxidants, astaxanthin, benefits, blood, body, brain, cholesterol, damage, deficiency, dha, disease, effects, epa, essential, fat, fatty, fish, food, health, healthy, heart, high, inflammation, inflammatory, krill, levels, nutrition, oil, omega, omega-3, phospholipid, powerful, products, protein, rates, red, side, skin, source, supplement, supplements, support, vitamins, weight

I checked these theme words against the pages ranked 1-10, 100-109, 200-209& 300-309. The results were interesting:

Position 1-10 on average used 77% of the theme words.

Position 100-109 on average used 66% of the theme words.

Position 200-209 on average used 69% of the theme words.

Position 300-309 on average used 75% of the theme words.

OK, we expected a high percentage of the theme words to be used in those pages ranked 300-309, because those are the pages that were used to collect the theme words. Those pages used an average of 75% of my theme words (remember I chose the words that only appeared on 7 or more pages, so that percentage sounds right).

However, look at the pages ranked 1-10. They actually used a higher percentage of theme words than the pages from which the theme words were collected! The top 10 pages used 77% of the theme words!

The pages ranked 100-109 and 200-209 where no slouches either. They used on average 66% and 69% of the theme words!

All of this goes to show that on average, ALL of the web pages that rank in Google are well themed around a set of "niche vocabulary". That is quite exciting, but also a little scary. If all of the pages ranked in Google are well-themed, chances are they are good quality, so how on earth do you beat them into the top 10? Well that is where you need to give your visitors what they want, and make it special. Give them something not offered by the other pages in the top 10. Make Google take notice of your content!

Before we leave these experiments, you might like to watch this video I created about Google and LSI:

http://ezseonews.com/lsivid2

How can you use this information to write better content?

If you are an expert in the field you are writing about, you will automatically and naturally use these theme words and phrases as you write about the topic. The truth is that you need to use these theme words and phrases if your article is to adequately cover the topic.

If however you are not an expert, then things are a little more difficult. You need to find which words and phrases are important to the topic you want to write about.

As you write the content sprinkle in relevant theme words and include a small number of highly relevant theme phrases. This will help the search engines identify the topic.

The theme phrases you use in a webpage should be the most important ones for that topic, as these will tell the search engines what that page is about. Do not under any circumstances use theme words or phrases more often than necessary. E.g. don't repeat a phrase 3 or 4 times simply because you want that page to rank for that term. Google's Penguin will be onto you and you could find your rankings drop for keyword stuffing or unnatural use of keywords.

Below is an example of a badly written article where theme phrases have been repeated solely for search engines. Ignoring the quality of the information in this piece, let's just look at an example of keyword stuffing:

DIY Architecture

Let's say you are planning a room addition. Did you know that you already possess the talents which allow you to calculate a comfortable size for the room addition? You may even possess some good design skills. Now you might think that I am wrong on this one.

For sake of discussion, let's assume that your local zoning ordinances will permit you to do just about anything. Some cities have strict setback lines and so forth that may limit the size of your planned addition - you must be aware of these limitations.

Go into your present living room. How does it feel? Imagine if it were say 6 feet wider and 8 feet longer. Maybe this size would allow you the space for that new couch, or a fireplace, built-in bookcases, whatever. The point is this. Use your existing rooms as starting points. You can measure them and stretch them to suit your needs. You need to start thinking in terms of space and how much you need.

Putting it on Paper

Remember earlier how I told you that my drafting skills were poor. Today, you don't need to know how to draw! If you have a fairly modern computer and sufficient memory, there are many affordable computer design programs that will draw your planned room addition.

I have highlighted one phrase that occurs three times (but I could have chosen a different example in this same article). The phrase is "room addition" and to me it sticks out because it is actually a little awkward to read, even unnatural when you read the text around it (which is fluff and padding). This looks a lot like a doorway page designed to rank for a single high demand, high profit keyword.

Checking the Google Keyword Planner confirms this:

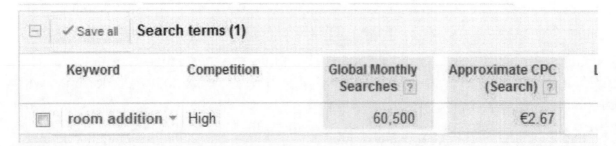

That phrase has 60,500 monthly searches, and costs advertisers around 2.67 Euros PER CLICK.

The "room addition" webmaster used AdSense advertising on the page, and that is further confirmation to me that he was creating doorway pages designed for the search engines to rank for single high-profit keywords.

Funnily enough, the site where this article is found used to be a site that Google showed off as a quality AdSense/Affiliate website (probably because of spectacular earnings in the Adsense program). During the initial rounds of Panda and Penguin, this site was penalized. This caused a lot of webmasters to conclude that Google does not like affiliate sites. After all, an affiliate site that Google once showcased as a shining example was itself penalized.

My view on this is that Google simply does not like poor or spammy content. This particular site was probably lucky to get away with its content for as long as it did, and most probably never got a real in-depth human review. When Google introduced Panda and Penguin, quality checks became automated, meaning EVERY site could now be thoroughly checked for quality. These checks obviously identified this and other pages on that site as low quality and in violation of the Google guidelines. On looking through a lot of the earlier content on that site, I'd agree that it was penalized for good reason. If I was that webmaster, my priority would be to remove all of the doorway pages and thin content on the site. While they remain, any penalty applied to the site will continue.

Finding Theme words & phrases

You have a couple of options when it comes to finding theme words for your content.

Option 1 - Google SERPs + SEOQuake

The first option is a 100% free option and involves using the Google SERPs together with a browser plugin called SEOQuake.

1. Install SEO Quake in your browser. There are versions for Firefox, Opera, Safari and Chrome.

2. Go to Google and search for the phrase you want to rank for.

3. Visit each of the top 10 pages in turn, and click the SEOQuake button to show the menu:

4. Select **Page Info** from that menu.

The resulting **page info** screen includes lists of keyword densities. We're not interested in the density itself, but rather what that density tells us about the importance of the word or phrase.

Here is a density report for my **health benefits of krill oil** search phrase:

Keywords density:

Total number of words: 3709

Keyword	Found in	Repeats	Density
krill	T, D, K	68	1.83%
oil	T, D, K	65	1.75%
view		42	1.13%
webmd	T, D	32	0.86%
health		27	0.73%
abstract		27	0.73%
treatments		18	0.49%
fatty		18	0.49%
acids		16	0.43%
information	D, K	14	0.38%
vitamin		14	0.38%
omega-3		13	0.35%
medical	D, K	12	0.32%
blood		12	0.32%
fish		11	0.30%
healthy		10	0.27%

It should be no surprise that this top ranked page includes the words "krill", "oil" and "health" in the top 5 most used words on the page.

You'll also find 2, 3 and 4 word phrases listed lower down the report.

By going through each of the top 10 pages and checking which words and phrases appear the most times, you can built up your own list of theme words and phrases to include in your own content.

Option 2 - Dedicated Tool

I wrote a tool that I personally use called Web Content Studio. Since it is my own tool, I do stand to profit from any sales, and therefore need to be upfront and transparent about it.

Since I do not want this book to be a sales pitch for my own tool, I won't be going into details on how to use it. Instead, I'll just list the main benefits and offer you a URL where you can check it out for yourself.

The main benefits of using Web Content Studio are:

1. The speed of finding niche vocabulary. Type in the phrase you want to rank for, and get WCS to return lists of words and phrases on the pages that rank in the top 10.

2. WCS will tell you how many of the top 10 pages each phrase appears on. This is important because a phrase that appears 100 times in the top 10 may appear 100 times on a single page, and not once on any of the other pages. The most important words appear on most of the top 10 pages, so these are the ones we need to target.

3. WCS has a WYSIWYG editor that allows you to create your content within the program, and then run reports to check the theme and quality of your work.

OK, that's enough on WCS. To see me using the WCS to write an article, visit this page:

http://ezseonews.com/writing-content/how-i-write-a-top-quality-article/

For more details on the tool itself, visit:

http://webcontentstudio.com

We now know the importance of the niche vocabulary in our content and how to find it. That will go a long way to making sure your article is quality. Understand the niche vocabulary in your chosen topic and use it naturally as you write your content.

There are a number of other on-page factors that you ned to get right. Let's look them.

On Page SEO factors to get right

The Title Tag

The title tag is probably the most important ranking factor on your page in terms of SEO benefits. It is also vital in terms of persuading Google searchers to click on your link. In the source code of your web page, the title tag looks like this:

<title>TITLE GOES HERE</title>

Search engines look at the words in your title tag to determine what your page is about. Therefore you should try to get your main keyword phrase into the title. The closer to the beginning of the title tag your keyword is, the better.

If I was writing a web page about the health benefits of krill oil, the important phrases in that search terms are: krill oil & health benefits.

If I do a search on Google for **health benefits of krill oil,** here are the title tags of the top 5 pages ranking for that term.

krill oil: Uses, Side Effects, Interactions and Warnings – WebMD

Krill Oil Benefits – Learn all the Wonderful **Benefits** of **Krill Oil**

Benefits of **Krill Oil** with Omega 3 Fats

Why **Krill Oil** Is Good for Your Heart | **Krill Oil Benefits**

Krill Oil: Benefits, Dangers & Side Effects - Drugs.com

All of these pages are authority pages in the health niche, so will have a massive ranking advantage over smaller sites, but you can still see they've included the main keywords in the title tag.

All 5 pages have the phrase **krill oil** near the beginning of the tag, and some duplicate that phrase at the end as well. Where possible, try to get the most important words near the start of the title tag.

The big omission in those titles is the word "health". Not one of those 5 pages include that word in their title tag, however, all 5 of these sites are massive health authority sites, so Google can pretty much assume the benefits refer to health.

Only the first page in the ranking does not use the words health or benefit(s), but that is WebMD, an authority site that Google trusts for all health related searches. The way Google has evolved over recent years means it can now accurately determine a searcher's intent. If someone searches for health benefits of krill oil, Google will understand that they are looking for the kind of information provided by that #1 ranked WebMD article.

When crafting your title tag, try to write a title that not only includes the words that make up your main phrase or concept, but something enticing so that people will want to click your link when they see the title.

Keep your title tag to **67 characters or less**. Any longer than that and it will be truncated in the search results.

Title tags on every page of your site should be unique. Never use the same title tag on two or more pages.

It is worth monitoring click through rates for your pages and tweaking the title tag to see if you can increase the CTR. Title and Meta Description are the two variables that you have the most control over in your quest for better CTR from the Google SERPs.

The Meta Description Tag

The Meta Description tag is not as important as the title tag, but you should still create a unique, interesting and enticing description on all of your pages. Google will often (though not always) use the Meta Description tag in the search results as the description of a listing.

In the source code of your web page, the Meta Description looks like this:

```
<meta name="description" content="DESCRIPTION GOES HERE."/>
```

Here are the Meta Descriptions of the top 5 pages ranking in Google for the krill oil term we used earlier.

1. Find patient medical information for **krill oil** on WebMD including its uses, effectiveness, side effects and safety, interactions, user ratings and products that have it.

2. **Krill Oil** will protect your heart, lower your cholesterol, relieve PMS symptoms, fight aging and inflammation, optimize your brain's capabilities, and boost your overall **health**!

3. **Krill oil** is one of the best sources of omega 3 fats, which greatly influence your gene expression and overall **health**.

4. **Krill oil** supplementation helps reduce triglyceride levels in adults, lowering your risk of heart disease.

5. **Krill Oil** information from Drugs.com, includes **Krill Oil** side effects, interactions and indications.

As you can see here, all 5 Meta Descriptions include the main keyword phrase **Krill Oil**. However, they don't use health or benefits as much as the page title. What you will see is other related words and phrases appearing, like **protect your heart, lower cholesterol, supplement/supplementation, risks, heart disease**, etc. These are some of the niche vocabulary for the search term, and it's a great idea to get some of the important vocabulary into the Meta Description (and title if you can fit it).

When I am creating a Meta Description, I always create it at the same time as I create the title tag. I want them to complement each other. I'll have a list of the most important words and phrases in a hierarchy, with the most important at the top. Top of my list for this search term would be **krill oil** and **health benefits** (or just benefits if my site was a health site). Lower down my list would be phrases like **lower triglycerides, heart health, side effects** etc.

The most important phrase (in this case krill oil) would go into both. The title would be written to include any other vital keywords related to the search term (like health benefits), while the Description would be used to include some of the niche vocabulary.

Together, the title and Meta Description would work together to cover the most important words and phrases related to my article.

The Meta Keyword Tag

The Meta Keyword tag is a place where you can list keywords related to your web page.

In the source code, it looks like this:

```
<meta name="keywords" content="Keyword1, keyword 2, etc">
```

A few years ago, search engines actually used the Meta Keyword tag as a ranking factor, and took notice of the words and phrases in this tag. Today, the search engines do not give you any boost in rankings for this tag. However, it is my belief that search engines may use this tag to spot spammers and award penalties.

Any page that has a keyword stuffed Meta Keyword tag IS breaking the webmaster guidelines laid down by Google, and I believe that pages doing this are penalized.

I personally do not use this tag on my sites and do not recommend you bother with it. If you do want to use it, make sure you only use a small number of keywords that are most related to your content AND that every single word or phrase you include in this tag is actually found on your web page.

Let's have a quick look at the Meta Keywords used by the top 5 sites for that krill oil search term.

1. krill oil, effectiveness, satisfaction, ease of use, uses, user ratings, user reviews, side effects, safety, interactions, medical information, medical advice, natural treatment, warnings, products

2. Does not use the Meta Keyword tag.

3. omega 3, krill oil, sources of omega 3, benefits of krill oil, omega 3 deficiency, omega 3 benefits, dha and epa

4. triglycerides, krill oi, triglyceride levels, krill oil vs fish oil, krill oil benefits

5. Krill Oil side effects

It is interesting to see that the pages ranked 3 and 4 are from the same website. Therefore Google is ranking 2 articles from the same site for the search term **health benefits of krill oil**. What I want you to look at are the title, Meta Description and keywords used for both of these articles.

See how they are unique, and tailored to the topic of the article? This is something you need to do on your own site. Every page, even if it is a similar topic to another page, MUST have a unique title, Meta description and Meta keywords (if you use them).

Headlines on your page

As a webmaster, you have control over the headlines in your content. You have several sizes of headlines, ranging from the biggest H1 header all the way down to the smallest H6 header.

In your web page source code, an H1 header looks like this:

<H1>HEADLINE HERE</H1>

In terms of user experience and SEO, I would recommend you only ever use H1, H2 and H3.

H1 is the main headline on your page, and because of this, the search engines give keywords in this heading the most attention. In SEO terms, your H1 headline is the one that has the biggest effect on your page ranking. However, just because it helps to rank your page, don't think you can use more than one. Only ever use one H1 header and put it at the top of your page as the opening title.

Try to get the main keyword for the page into the H1 header, preferably near the start of the headline.

As you write your content, break it up with H2 headers. If an H2 section has sub-sections, use H3s for those titles. I rarely use H3 headers on my pages as H1 and H2 are sufficient in nearly every case. Be aware that H2 and H3 have very little effect on rankings, so I don't recommend you try to add keywords to these unless it makes sense to do so. Just don't go out of your way to add them.

The opening H1 headers of my top 5 pages ranking for **health benefits of krill oil** are:

1. Find a Vitamin or Supplement

2. Exciting **Krill Oil Benefits** That Make You **Healthier**, Happier, Younger and Stronger!

3. **Krill Oil:** This Almost Perfect Natural Oil Could Slow Down Your Aging Clock

4. **Krill Oil** Supplementation Lowers Your Triglycerides

5. **Krill Oil**

The page ranked #1 (WebMD) is again the odd one out here due mainly to its authority, making it rank more easily. It does use a second H1 right under the first one, and that one is **Krill Oil**. I don't recommend you create two H1 headers on a page, but this site gets away with it because of Google's tolerance for authority sites.

As you can see from the other 4 pages, the H1 headers all include **Krill Oil** near the beginning of the headline. We've also got other niche vocabulary appearing in these headlines.

When creating your headlines, put your main keyword phrase into the headline near the beginning if possible. Make sure your headlines read well for your visitors.

Image optimization

When you add an image to your page, the source code (in its simplest form) looks like this:

```
<img src="IMAGE URL" alt="ALT TEXT" />
```

You might also have width and height parameters.

The **Image URL** in that code will be the URL to the image (which includes the image filename). Google can read the image filename in this URL, so it makes sense to help Google out and tell them what the image is. If the image is a bottle of krill oil, call the file "bottle-of-krill-oil.jpg". If it's an image of krill in the sea, call it "krill-swimming-in-sea.jpg", or whatever helps describe the image. The opportunity is clearly here to insert a keyword, but don't overdo it. Only insert the most important word or phrase.

The other important part of this code is the ALT text. This is the text shown in browsers when images are turned off. It's also the text that is read by text-to-speech software often used by those with sight impairment. Use the ALT tag to describe the image for these users. You can put a keyword in there, but don't stuff.

A couple of the top 5 pages in Google ranking for health benefits of krill oil have used images. Let's look at the source code of those images (I'll clean up the HTML code so you can only see the filename and ALT tag):

1. <img src="/**krill-oil-hand**.jpg" alt="**krill-oil-hand**">

2. <img src=" /**krill-oil-beats-common-diseases**.jpg" alt="**krill oil beats common diseases**">

You'll notice that the filename and the ALT tag in each example are the same. This is fine and I actually recommend you do this.

You may want to experiment by creating a different filename and ALT tag for an image. However, if you do, I recommend you do not use different keywords in each. Both of these should contain the same description, one for the search engine and the other for visually impaired users. If Google think you are trying to get different keywords into the filename and ALT tags of the same image, they might label you a spammer. At the end of the day, it's just easier to use the same sentence for filename and ALT tag, and it looks natural.

Spelling & Grammar

If spelling and grammar are bad on your site, visitors will not be overly impressed. This can lead to higher bounce rates and lower time on site. For no other reason that this, it's a good idea to check both.

Google will see spelling and grammar as quality signals. The odd mistake won't make a difference, but pages with lots of mistakes will probably not rank well in the long-term. A site that has lots of pages with poor grammar and spelling is unlikely to rank for anything.

Links on the page

Your web page will include links to other web pages. These web pages may be on the same site (internal links), or pages on a different site (external links).

Over time, web pages can be moved or deleted, so it is important to check links periodically to make sure your links are not broken.

The most common broken links on a page tend to be external links, since we have no control over pages that are run by other webmasters. They can remove or rename a page without notice, and when they do, your link is broken.

Fortunately, there is a good free tool that can check for broken links on your site. It's called Xenu Link Sleuth.

http://home.snafu.de/tilman/xenulink.html

This tool will find all broken links, both internal and external.

Internal links on your site can also get broken if you rename a page, or delete one. I use a lot of internal linking on my sites to help my visitors, and help Google spider my content. Changing a filename of a page could break dozens of links. To prevent this, I use an internal linking plugin that automates the linking of words and phrases to pages. If I rename or delete a page, I can simply change the settings in the internal linking plugin and all internal links on my site are updated automatically.

You can read more about the internal linking plugin that I use, and how I go about internal linking here:

http://ezseonews.com/int-link

But what about linking out to other websites? Is that a good or bad idea?

Linking to other websites is natural. Think about writing a research paper for a minute. It's natural to cite other papers.

Similarly, when you create an article for your site, it's natural to "cite" other web pages by linking to them. These might be pages you used for research, or pages you found interesting and relevant to your own content. In other words, they are pages that you think your visitors would appreciate you sharing.

The one thing you need to be aware of is that links to other pages are votes for those pages. If those other pages are spammy or low quality, those links can actually hurt you because Google assumes you are voting for spam.

Therefore, if you link to a page that you don't necessarily endorse, it is important to use the nofollow tag in the link.

The source code of a link with the nofollow tag looks like this.

```
<a href="Theothersite.com" rel="nofollow">The Other Site</a>
```

I "nofollow" all outbound links in my content unless it is a recognized authority site in my niche. Then I'll usually leave the nofollow out because I want Google to associate my site with these authority sites.

While we are on the subject of nofollow, if you allow visitors to comment on your content, make their links nofollow. That includes any link used in the comment itself, and the URL that is often allowed to their own site.

This may cut down on the number of comments you get because other webmasters see very little in it for them. However, if you don't do this, you'll quickly find that as the comments build up, you have dozens and then hundreds of outbound links to pages you have no control over and no idea of quality. Getting a Google penalty would likely be only a matter of time.

Spying on competitors for content ideas

One of my favourite ways of generating content ideas is to spy on my competitors and see what they are adding to their website.

The easy way of doing this is to subscribe to your competitor's RSS feed, and monitor that for new content.

If you collect RSS feeds from several competitors, you can enter them all into a single "collection" in a service like Feedly. Feedly will then notify you of all new content across all of the sites.

You can see I have added three feeds related to juicing into a collection called "Juicing". If I click on the "Juicing" item in the menu, it shows me new content from all of those feeds in the collection:

Juicing
17 unread articles

 Q Search

TODAY

Hot Spiced Apple Cider Juicer Recipe
As the weather is cooling off, there are not many better ways to heat up on a cool evening than a hot spiced apple cider. This juicing recipe allows you to enjoy this delicious treat but also have the benefits of juicing at the same time.
Juicing for Weight Loss / 1h

YESTERDAY

Appetizing Turnip Juice
The nutrients supplied by the juice of turnip root and its greens offer an ideal way for "powering up." The vegetable provides a large variety of essential vitamins, minerals and fiber.
Juicing the Rainbow / by Andy Williams / 19h

NOV 27

Spicy Green Metabolism Boosting Juicing Recipe
You have probably heard that hot peppers can help boost your metabolism and help support fat burning... here is a recipe to give your body a calorie burning boost and is also a fantastic green juicing recipe great for detoxing
Juicing for Weight Loss / 4d

This is a great way to find new content ideas. Let your competitors do the research to find out what their readers want, then apply their ideas to your own site. An upside of this is that you can be the first to go and comment on their new articles, and that can lead to more traffic to your own site.

This method can be extended by using Google Alerts to monitor keywords in your niche. If for example you had a website about bee colony collapse, you could set up an alert at Google so that whenever a new item appears in the SERPs that is related to bee colony collapse, you'd be notified. Notifications can be sent via email, or they can be included in an RSS feeds which you can add to your Feedly account. Once set up, you have your finger on the pulse in your niche and any breaking news would be delivered straight to you, ready for your own "breaking news" article that you could post on your site. Share this story via social media, and you can quickly find these articles attracting backlinks and traffic.

The topic of web content could fill a book in its own right. In fact, I have written a book called "Creating Fat Content" which extends the ideas here, and is available on Amazon. See section at the end of this book if you want a link.

2. Site organization

What Google tells us about site design

Google gives us a lot of information about site design which we should consider best practices. Put another way, Google knows how their search engine works, and therefore knows the site design elements that work best with Google.

These are all listed on the Google Webmaster Guidelines, but let's go through some of the important points.

1. Create a sitemap

Google wants you to create a sitemap to submit to Google Webmaster Tools, and I recommend you do this. If you are using Wordpress, there are a lot of plugins that can create these for you.

Google also suggests you have a sitemap for visitors to help guide them to relevant parts of the site. I actually think that this is less important than the sitemap for the search engines, since a good navigation system on the site (plus a good search facility) will do that job for you. It is my experience that users would rather use an intuitive navigation system that effortlessly guides them through the site, than a long list of URLs in a sitemap.

2. Make sure your site has a clear hierarchy

We'll look at the hierarchical structure of the site very soon, but for now, just know that Google expects EVERY page on your site to be reachable through a static link on another page (and not necessarily the sitemap). I'd go one step further in suggesting that every page on your site should be no more than two clicks from the homepage, with important pages being only one click from the homepage.

3. Keep links on a page to a reasonable number

Search engines can actually spider every link on a page, even very long ones, so I can only assume this guideline is for the benefit of users. If you have certain calls to action that you want visitors to make, fewer links (and other distractions) are certainly a good idea.

4. Dynamic pages v static pages

Dynamic pages often contain the "?" character before some parameters. Google suggests you try to make static rather than dynamic pages, though if you have to use dynamic pages, try to keep the parameters to a bare minimum.

5. A robots.txt file?

Robot.txt files can be used to set rules for your site, e.g. stopping search engine spiders from crawling specific pages, effectively hiding them from the SERPs.

A robots.txt file sits in the root folder of your site and basically contains a series of allow or disallow commands, telling spiders/crawlers which pages they can and cannot access. Google suggests that if you have pages on your site that you do not want spiders to crawl, use a robots.txt file. If on the other hand you want the spiders to crawl every page, do not create a robot.txt file, not even a blank one.

6. Check your site in different browsers

Different web browsers can display a page very differently. It is therefore wise to check your site in a range of different browsers to make sure it looks good for everyone (or at least the vast majority of your visitors).

Do a Google search for **browser compatibility testing** for various free services that allow you to test your site in a variety of browsers.

At the very minimum, you should check in mobile browsers. A responsive theme is a must these days. Responsive themes adjust how your site is displayed depending on the browser resolution of the visitor. At the time of writing this, between 45% - 60% of my own site visitors (for a variety of sites) are coming in on mobile devices.

For Wordpress users, I used to recommend a plugin that switched themes for mobile users. However, the themes it produced were a little crude and I now recommend you buy a responsive theme. I personally use the Genesis theme framework. You can see a range of themes that use Genesis here:

http://ezseonews.com/studiopress

On that page, click the "Shop for Themes" link in the top navigation menu.

Look for the themes that are labelled **HTML 5** as these are the responsive ones. You can click those theme thumbnails to get more details of the theme, and see a demo of each one.

Try loading some of those themes in your desktop computer, your tablet and your phone. See how each theme changes the site design according to the screen dimensions of your device?

This type of responsive theme will keep mobile users happy, without compromising the experience of desktop visitors.

7. Monitor your site load times

Site visitors will not hang around if your pages take a long time to load. Therefore don't add unnecessary bloat to your pages. Create light, fast-loading pages with optimized images to make sure your pages load as quickly as possible. Page load speed is certainly a factor used in the Google algorithm, though it is not a major one.

I personally use a free service for checking page load speeds. It's over at

http://gtmetrix.com

We'll come back and look at this tool later.

OK, those are the guidelines from Google specifically about site structure. I recommend you head on over to the Google Webmaster Guidelines and study them. They'll help keep you on the right side of Google.

A note about Exact Match Domain names

An exact match domain (EMD) is one that is basically using the main keyword phrase you are targeting as the domain name, e.g. buyviagraonline.com (if you wanted to target "buy Viagra online"). Typically, EMD websites target very few keywords, with all eggs being placed firmly in the "EMD phrase" basket.

If you are starting a new website, choosing a domain name will be the first task you'll need to do. Many people who teach SEO will tell you to go for an EMD because it offers ranking advantages over non-EMDs. This was true in the past, but not now. In fact, on September 28th 2012, Google released an update that was meant to reduce the ranking ability of poor quality EMDs. You can read the announcement by Matt Cutts (Google's head of spam) on Twitter:

https://twitter.com/mattcutts/status/251789327691042816

This shouldn't have come as a surprise to the better SEOs, because 2 years earlier, Matt Cutts announced that Google would be looking at why EMDs ranked so well when he spoke at Pubcon in November 2010.

The problem with EMDs today is that they are scrutinized by Google. It will probably take a lot less to get an EMD site penalized; therefore I recommend you look for a brandable domain name instead. Find a domain name that people will remember.

What is a low quality EMD?

I would say that any EMD that is not a brand or company name is at risk of being labeled low quality. The reason is simply that EMDs are chosen by webmasters to rank for a particular phrase.

Webmasters have traditionally looked at their keyword research, found a phrase that is commercially attractive (low competition, high search volume, high AdWords Cost per click) and registered the phrase as an EMD with the intention of ranking for that phrase and monetizing with Google AdSense. Any website that is setup with the primary goal of ranking for a single phrase is a glorified doorway page, and we know what Google thinks of those.

One thing that makes a lot of these low quality EMDs stand out is the high percentage of backlinks that use the exact same keyword phrase as anchor text. The problem for EMD owners is that using that phrase is natural, because it's the name of the website. This is why I suggest you avoid them, unless it is your company/brand name.

Summary: Any EMD that has obviously been chosen solely for it potential profit is likely to have problems going forward.

Good site structure

The way you structure your site is extremely important not only for the search engines but also human visitors. Good organization coupled with a clear and intuitive navigation system is vital.

From a human point of view, it makes sense that content on a similar topic should all be found in the same section of the site. For example, if you have a website selling bicycles, all of the mountain bikes should be found together, all of the road bikes in another section, and maybe bikes for children in another section.

If a 22 year old mountain bike rider came to your site, she should be able to browse the mountain bike stuff without seeing road racers or children's bicycles.

If you're using WordPress as a site builder, organizing your site like this is extremely easy. You simply create a category for each section, and assign posts to the most logical category. While it is possible to assign a post to more than one category, I recommend each post should only be put into one, as this makes for a tighter organization (a better silo). If you need to further categorize your articles, e.g. having all 26 inch frame bikes on the same page, use tags instead of additional categories for the frame sizes. We'll look at tags a little later.

This type of "silo" structure works very well for the search engines because it helps them categorize your content. Think of a site that has reviews on the following bikes and accessories.

- Allen Deluxe 4-Bike Hitch Mount Rack
- GMC Denali Pro Road Bike
- GMC Denali Women's Road Bike

- GMC Topkick Dual-Suspension Mountain Bike

- Hollywood Racks E3 Express 3-Bike Trunk Mount Rack

- Kawasaki DX226FS 26-Inch Dual Suspension Mountain Bike

- Mongoose Exile Dual-Suspension Mountain Bike

- Pacific Stratus Men's Mountain Bike

- Topeak Explorer Bike Rack

- Victory Vision Men's Road Bike

If you were to put these into related group (silos), those silos would look something like this.

Silo 1 Mountain Bikes

GMC Topkick Dual-Suspension Mountain Bike

Kawasaki DX226FS 26-Inch Dual Suspension Mountain Bike

Mongoose Exile Dual-Suspension Mountain Bike

Pacific Stratus Men's Mountain Bike

Silo 2 Road Bikes

GMC Denali Pro Road Bike

GMC Denali Women's Road Bike

Victory Vision Men's Road Bike

Silo 3 Car Racks

Allen Deluxe 4-Bike Hitch Mount Rack

Hollywood Racks E3 Express 3-Bike Trunk Mount Rack

Topeak Explorer Bike Rack

So the overall structure of the site would be:

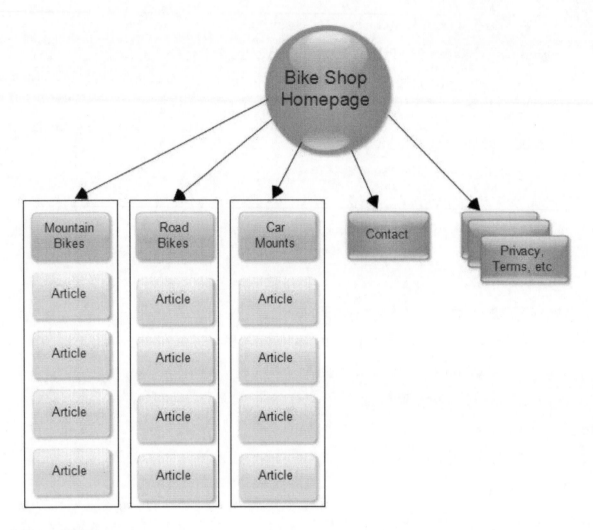

Internal links

One of the most overlooked pieces of the SEO puzzle is internal linking. This not only helps the search engines spider your pages, but it also helps visitors find other related content within your site.

With WordPress, there are plugins that can help you automate some of the internal linking on your site. For example "Yet Another Related Posts" plugin, or YARP to its friends, is a free WordPress plugin that will automatically create a related posts section at the end of every article on your site. You can configure it so that it can only find related posts within the same category, and this can help create a tighter, more natural silo with articles linking out to related content on your site.

Here is an example of a "Related Posts" section created by YARP:

Related Posts

› Curcumin, the powerful antioxidant found in Turmeric
Turmeric contains an active ingredient called Curcumin. This active agent has amazing health benefits.

› Turmeric as a powerful antioxidant
Turmeric contains curcumin, a powerful antioxidant. In this video, Dr. Mercola discusses the benefits and properties of curcumin.

This example shows related posts in the sidebar of a site. However, a great place to include them is at the end of an article. That way, when your visitor finished reading one article, they immediately see a list of related articles that might also interest them, keeping them on your site for longer.

Linking pages on a site together

Another form of internal linking, which I think is extremely important, is links within the body of your articles.

For example, if you are writing an article about the "GMC Topkick Dual-Suspension Mountain Bike", you might like to compare certain features of the bike to the "Mongoose Exile Dual-Suspension Mountain Bike". When you mention the name of the Mongoose Exile bike, it would help your visitors if you linked that phrase to your Mongoose Exile review. This would also help the search engines find that article, and help them determine what it is about (based on the link text).

This type of internal linking helps to increase indexing of your site as well as the rankings of individual pages.

To read more about internal linking, I recommend you read

Internal Linking & SEO

http://ezseonews.com/backlinks/internal-linking-seo/

Tags - another way to categorize your content

Tags are another way to categorize content if you are running a WordPress site. When you write a post, you can include a number of these tags which can help further categorize it.

For example, if you wrote a post about the "Dyson DC 33 Animal" vacuum, you would probably put it in the category "Dyson", as that is the most logical "navigation label" for your visitors.

However, you might also want to offer your visitors an easy way to find vacuums that use the Dyson Ball technology, or contain a HEPA filter. Rather than have a category for "Dyson Ball" and another for "HEPA filter" (and put the DC33 animal in all three categories), a better way would be to create tags for this extra classification.

For example, here are some tags you might use on the vacuum site:

- Upright
- Dyson Ball
- Pet hair
- HEPA filter
- Bagless

These tags will help to categorize the posts within the Dyson category (and every other category on your site).

WordPress actually creates a page for each of these tags, and each of these tag pages can actually rank quite well in Google.

Let's look at an example.

These four vacuums all have a HEPA filter:

1. Eureka Boss Smart-Vac Upright.
2. Hoover Windtunnel
3. BISSELL Cleanview Helix Upright Vacuum Cleaner
4. Miele S2 Series Lightweight

The first vacuum will be in the Eureka CATEGORY with all other Eureka vacuums.

The second vacuum will be in the Hoover CATEGORY with all other Hoover vacuums.

The third vacuum will be in the Bissell CATEGORY and the fourth vacuum will be in the Miele CATEGORY.

However, all 4 vacuums would be tagged with "HEPA filter", so would also appear on the HEPA Filter "tag page".

In addition, the first three would also appear on the "Upright" tag.

When people visit your site, they'll be able to narrow down their choice by Brand (using category navigation), or by looking for specific features (using tags to navigate).

WARNING

I advise that you use tags wisely. Don't tag every post with hundreds of tags. Think about your tags and only include the most relevant ones for each post.

Use and abuse of tags

A lot of people do not really understand the significance of tags, and see them as a "keyword list" similar to the Meta Keywords tag. To that end, they create long tag lists for each post. Here is a screenshot of some tags assigned to one post I saw:

Tags: advantages disadvantages of solar power, advantages of a solar panels, advantages of solar cell panel, are MONOCRYSTALLINE sollar pannels good, best mono solar panel price, best quality monocrystaline solar panels, bestpv panels mono or poly, buy pv panels monocrystalline, compare monocrystalin policrystalin photovoltaic, compare monocrystalline and polycrystalline, compare monocrystalline and polycrystalline pannel, compare pollycrystalline vs. monocrystaline modules, crystal cells for solar panels, crystal solar, crystalline si solar efficiency, crystalline solar best, crystalline solar cell technology, crystalline solar cells cost, crystalline solar panels, crystalline solar plate cost, crystalline solar pv module, csun mono-crystalline panels, describe 2 advantages of solar cells, difference between mono and polycrystalline, difference between monocrystalline, difference monocrystalline polycrystalline solar, difference solar panels polycrystalline &, disadvantage to many solar panels, ecokes monocrystalline, ecokes photovoltaic panels, ecokes solar panel, electricity, energy, how i get Monocrystalline silicon, how many rating monocrystalline cell, how Monocrystalline cells are made, how to produce monocrytaline silicon, http://www.monocrystal photo cells/, is monocrystalline better than polycrystalline, is monocrystalline PV best, LUXOR Solar Mono Crystal Dickschichtmodule, maker of monocrystalline panels, mon vs poly efficiency, mono and poly crystalline, mono crystalline pv panels, mono or poly solar panels, mono silicon solar panels, mono solar panel dimensions, mono solar power, mono v poly solar panels, mono versus poly crystalling panels, mono vs poly crystalline panels, mono vs. multicrystalline solar panel, Mono-

That was actually only about 25% of the tags listed on that page. They just kept scrolling down the page.

In SEO terms, this is bad practice. Very bad!

To understand why long tag lists are a bad idea, let's look at what happens when you create a post.

When you publish a post on your blog, WordPress will put that post onto several pages of your site including:

1. A page specially created to show the post.
2. The category page.
3. The author page.

4. For every tag assigned to the post, the post will appear on the corresponding tag page. Tag a post with 25 tags, and that article will be duplicated across 25 tag pages!

Can you see how that one post can be duplicated on multiple pages of your site?

Duplicate content on a site is NOT a good thing!

Another big problem with using lots of tags occurs when a particular tag is only used for one post. In that case, the tag page will only have the one article on it, meaning it is almost identical to the post page created by WordPress for that article.

How to use WordPress tags properly

Get into the tag mindset! Before you use a tag on a post, think about the tag page that will be created for that tag.

Your article will appear on each of those tag pages. Is that what you want? Is this tag going to be used on other relevant posts? Never use a tag if it will not be used by several other posts on your site.

With this in mind, here is what I suggest you do:

During the design stages of your site, make a list on a piece of paper of all the tags you want to use on your site (you can add/edit this list as you build out your site, but have a list you can refer to). As you create posts on your site, refer to the tag list you wrote down, and use only tags on that list. By all means add new tags over time, but make sure that tags are going to be used more than once. Don't create a tag that will only ever be used on a single post on your site. Also, only use a few of the most relevant tags for each post.

Finally, never use a word or phrase for a tag that is (or will be) a category name.

After all, WordPress will create pages for each category as well; so think of tags as an "additional" categorization tool at your disposal.

What if my site already has a lot of posts with spammy tags?

Fortunately there are a number of good plugins to help manage tags if you work with WordPress. Just visit the Plugin directory and search for "Tag Manager". Choose one that has good reviews and works with the current version of Wordpress.

Modifying tag pages?

Quite often you'll find that your tag pages are getting traffic from Google. I have found that the tag pages often rank very well for the chosen tag (as a keyword phrase).

I like to modify my tag pages (and category pages) by adding an introductory paragraph to each one. The Genesis theme templates have a built in feature that makes it easy, for both tag pages and category pages.

http://ezseonews.com/genesis

Created this way, the tag pages have an introduction, followed by a list of all related articles (those which have been tagged with that particular tag). This helps to make your tag pages unique, but also allows you to add more value to your site.

Used properly, tag pages can work for you. Used without thought, tag pages can increase duplicate content on your site and increase your chances of getting penalized by Google.

3. Authority

What is an Authority Site?

If you go over to the Free Dictionary website and search for authority, there are a lot of different definitions. This definition is probably most apt with regards to websites:

au·thor·i·ty (ə-thôr'ĭ-tē, ə-thŏr'-, ô-thôr'-, ô-thŏr'-)
n. pl. **au·thor·i·ties**
1.
  a. The power to enforce laws, exact obedience, command, determine, or judge.
  b. One that is invested with this power, especially a government or body of government officials: *land titles issued by the civil authority.*
2. Power assigned to another; authorization: *Deputies were given authority to make arrests.*
3. A public agency or corporation with administrative powers in a specified field: *a city transit authority.*
4.
  a. An accepted source of expert information or advice: *a noted authority on birds; a reference book often cited as an authority.*
  b. A quotation or citation from such a source: *biblical authorities for a moral argument.*

To make your website an authority site, it has to be an **"accepted source of expert information or advice"**.

A well-organized site with excellent content is a great start (the first two pillars of good SEO). However those two pillars are not enough to make your site an authority, because no-one will have heard about you or your great site.

Your site (or your own name if YOU personally want to be the authority) MUST be well-known in your particular niche.

So how do you get well known?

Answering that is the easy part - *you need to put your site name and face out there on as many relevant, high quality places as you can, with links pointing back to relevant pages on your site*.

In other words, backlinks. This use to be easy, but with Penguin on the prowl, backlinks is an area that can quickly get you penalized; especially if your site is relatively new or doesn't have much authority yet.

There is another aspect of this I want to discuss before we go into details on backlinking, and that is linking out from your site to authority sites in your niche. We have talked about this earlier in the book, but I want to bring it up again, just to reinforce the point.

We are all part of a huge web of interlinked websites. If you were talking about something in your niche, doesn't it make sense that you might make references to other authority sites?

e.g. If a search engine was trying to evaluate your page on the Atkins Diet, don't you think that links to other peoples studies on the diet, as well as medical references, etc. would help make your page more of an authority? Sure it would, as long as your own content was also excellent. It would also help instill confidence in your visitor by giving them more value.

So when you are writing content for your website, don't be afraid to link to other authority sites if they have relevant information. Don't use "nofollow" on links to well-known authority sites, as that just tells the search engine you:

(a) Don't trust the site you are linking to, or
(b) You are trying to hoard the link juice on your own site.

I recommend you open these links in a new window so that your visitors are not taken away from your site if they click these links. What you may even decide to do is have a reference section at the end of your post, with active hyperlinks pointing to other authority sites.

In short, link out to other authority sites - but only when it makes sense and you think it will help your visitor.

OK, outbound links are sorted.

What about the links coming into your site?

Backlinks to a website are a very important part of the Google algorithm. It's the main reason webmasters build links to their own websites – to help them rank better. However, there is something very important that you need to know about link building. It's not something that most SEO book or courses will tell you, mainly because they want to sell you their link building tools, or get you to buy recommended tools through their affiliate links. It's this:

Google don't want you building links to your site.

In fact, we can probably state it a little more strongly than that.

Google hate you building links to your site.

Google are on the warpath against "webspam" and "link schemes", and that includes "unnatural" links. Any link that was created purely to help your page rank higher in the SERPs, and/or YOU have control over, is an **unnatural link**.

Properties of an unnatural link include any link where you, the webmaster:

1. Chose the link text.

2. Chose the destination page.

3. Chose which page the link appears on.

4. Chose where on the page the link appears.

So is every link you have built to your site unnatural?

Well, actually no. Any link that you create, and would have created even if the search engines did not exist, is not unnatural.

An example of this is if you write an article for an authority site and put a link to your site in the bio. That's a natural link to put, since you are the expert that wrote the article and people want to know where they can find out more about you. You would put that link in there even if there were no search engines, wouldn't you?

The term unnatural is used by Google to describe those links you created to boost the rank of your page in the SERPs. It's a fine dividing line. However, the penalties for crossing the line can be severe.

If Google find links that you have created to your site, with the sole purpose of helping your site rank better, they will ignore those links at best, but are probably more likely to actively penalize your site.

You need to bear this in mind as you build links to your web pages.

It can be tempting to go over to the dark side of SEO. There are a lot of people out there that will show you proof of the benefits of keyword-rich anchor text links (usually just before selling you a link-building tool or service). What they don't show you is what happens to that page in the long-term. This type of link can still give good results in the short-term, but only until Google catch you (and in 2015, it is automated software that hunts you down, and it is very efficient).

In this book, I'll only cover what I consider to be the best long-term strategies for link building; those that look natural to Google.

Here is the general concept of link building:

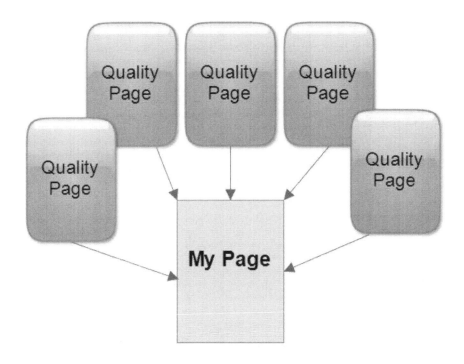

Search Rankings Increase

As you build quality links to your page, your page will move up the search engine rankings.

Some people will tell you that it doesn't matter whether inbound links are on related pages (to your page) or not. That may have been the case several years ago, but it certainly is not the case now.

If you had a website on "breeding goldfish" and you had 100 inbound links to your site, but 95% of those were on pages that talked about things like:

- Prescription drugs

- Viagra

- Auto maintenance

- Wedding speeches

- Golf Equipment

- Etc

What is that telling the search engines?

I think Google would look at these backlinks and conclude you were involved in backlinking schemes to help your pages rank better. As we saw earlier, Google's webmaster guidelines tell us that this is a quick road to a penalty.

If the search engines want to use inbound links as a measure of authority, then surely the most authoritative links you could get would be from quality pages that were on a similar topic to the page they link to?

With Google Penguin, this may be even more important as Google appears to be giving less weight to the anchor text and more to the actual THEME of the webpage (or site) that the link is on. Therefore, look for links from pages and sites that are relevant to your own, and look for quality sites to get your links on.

Always consider quality in every backlink you get.

The backlink should be on a quality page, on a quality site. The page on your site should also be quality.

What I have described is a little scary. If bad backlinks can get your site penalized, then what is to stop your competitors building backlinks to you site? This happens, and is called **negative SEO**.

Is Negative SEO real?

Negative SEO is a term that refers to webmasters/SEOs who build poor quality links to a competitor's website in an effort to get it penalized. Many SEOs agree that since Penguin, negative SEO is a reality. I actually think it was a reality even before Panda, and one of my own tests certainly provided some evidence.

At the start of the 2011 (before Panda) I started some aggressive backlinking to a site of mine that was several years old. I wanted to use this as a test, so I set up about 150 blogs (using automation software) that I could use to get backlinks from. Since I controlled these blogs, I controlled the backlinks and had the power to delete them if I needed to.

I started submitting content to these 150 sites, with backlinks going to the pages on my test site.

The rankings climbed for several weeks, and so did my traffic. I was monitoring my page rankings for 85 keywords, and around 60 had reached the top 10 in Google, with a large proportion in the top 3.

Then, I woke up one morning to find that my site had been penalized. All 85 keywords dropped out of the top 100.

They stayed out of the top 100 for 8 weeks. I then started phase two of my test. I deleted all 150 blogs, thereby eliminating all of those spammy backlinks.

Over the next month, things started to slowly improve. Pages started climbing back into the top 100 to the point where I ended up with 64 of the 85 phrases back in the top 100. Around 42 pages were back in the top 30, and 12 were back in the top 10.

NOTE: Obviously my rankings did not return to pre-penalty levels, because they were only at those pre-penalty levels because of the backlinks I had built. However, I think it was fairly clear that my site penalty had been lifted.

I also know that the penalty was applied by the algorithm and not a human reviewer. When a site gets penalized by a human reviewer, you have to submit a re-inclusion request after cleaning up the problems. I didn't have to do that, and when the backlinks were cleaned up, rankings returned.

If your site gets penalized today, chances are it is an algorithmic penalty like in my example. Fixing the issues will remove the penalty and that is actually great news.

Here is a diagram showing poor backlinks to a page:

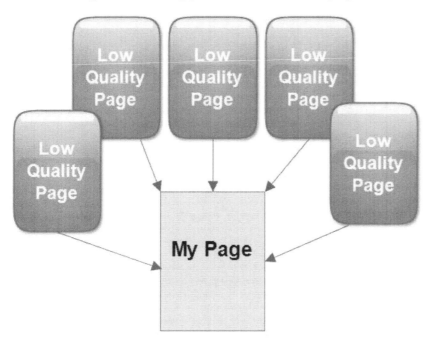

In this model, poor backlinks actually cause YOUR page to get penalized and drop down the rankings.

The point to take home from this is to concentrate on backlinks from good authority sites.

What type of backlinks can you get?

First and foremost, go for QUALITY, not quantity.

To be seen as a real authority, your site needs incoming links from other authority sites. Since Google Penguin, I no longer recommend using any type of automated link building tool.

WHAT?????

I know, I know....

"If I cannot use automated link building tools, how can I get enough links to rank well?"

To answer that question, let me ask you one thing.

Do you believe your page DESERVES to rank well based on the **quality of the content** and the **authority of you/your site**?

If you answer no, then you will have to go down the black hat SEO path to get your page ranked, and ultimately that path will lead to penalties, lost rankings and starting all over again when Google catches up with you.

For a page to rank well on your site, you need to make sure it **deserves** to rank well (in terms of content and your site/author authority).

Think of this example.

You write a page on the "health benefits of vitamin D".

Do you think your page deserves to rank above medical sites, where the authors are medical doctors? Why? Google clearly wants to show the most useful and accurate information it can to its visitors, and that probably means choosing a medical authority site over yours, even if your content is better. You cannot compete on the authority level unless you are an authority on the "health benefits of vitamin D" and that is the way it should be.

How might you gain authority in this area? Well quite simply, you could write articles on vitamin D and have them posted on numerous authority sites, with a link back to your site/page in the resource box. Don't try to stick keywords into your backlinks. Use only the title of your site, or the title of the article you are linking to, or the bare URL of the page you are linking to.

When you think about it in these terms, can you understand why I say abandon automated link builders? The links coming into your pages need to be of the utmost quality and professionalism. They need to build your authority, not ruin it by having some computer-generated article with your name on it linking back to your site.

So, with the idea of quality firmly planted in your mind, let me suggest a few places you can get content published that might actually build your reputation and authority. Before I do that though, I would like to give two general guidelines for backlinking.

1. Only look to get links on authority sites that are related to your own niche.
2. Try to be EVERYWHERE. Whenever someone is searching for information in your niche, make sure they constantly see your name or site cropping up.

It doesn't matter if your link is on a Page Rank zero page, as long as that page resides on a site that has good authority. Two of the only indicators we have for authority are domain age and domain Page Rank, so I suggest you use these while you can (Page Rank may well be disappearing soon) . Look for domains that are 5+ years old, with domain Page Rank of 4 or more and you should be safe.

Anchor text?

With Google Penguin, things have changes a lot.

You used to optimize a webpage by including the main keyword phrase in the page title, URL, H1 header and several times in the content. We'd then point a lot of backlinks to the page using the main keyword phrase as the anchor text.

Google used to reward this type of optimization.

Then came the Penguin, and as we've seen, that type of optimization is more likely to get your page/site penalized.

As well as de-optimizing on-page factors, we have had to de-optimize backlinks to our pages. In fact, if you check out the Google Webmaster Guidelines, you'll see this as an example of a "link scheme":

Links with optimized anchor text in articles or press releases distributed on other sites. For example:
There are many wedding rings on the market. If you want to have a wedding, you will have to pick the best ring. You will also need to buy flowers and a wedding dress.

Google are clearly cracking down on keyword-rich anchor text links that point to a webpage. This type of backlinking used to be the norm, but when we look at those links; they really do look spammy, don't they?

Today we need to be smarter about our backlinks. If we want to survive Google Penguin (and all future algorithm updates), then we cannot create backlinks like this. These are the typical types of backlinks created by automated software tools, so that's another compelling reason not to use software to generate backlinks.

NOTE: I don't believe that Google will penalize a web page that has a few backlinks like this. For example, if your web page was about dog training, and 1% of your incoming backlinks used the anchor text "dog training collars", I think that would be

OK. However, if 50% of your backlinks used "dog training collars" as anchor text, then that would be an issue.

The Google tolerance for this type of link has been shifting. Google seem to be losing all patience for keyword rich anchor text, especially in the body of an article on another website. I would suggest that it is now dangerous to have even 10% of the links to a specific page use the same keyword phrase. Tomorrow, next week or next year, that might drop to 5%, who knows?

Over time, Google is becoming less tolerant (and with the disavow tool, Google can do this with a clear conscience). At the start of 2013, a study was released showing this tolerance shift. The study showed that:

1. When Penguin was first released, Google did not penalize sites even when 90% of incoming links were spammy.

2. By June 2012, Google would only tolerate 65% spammy links before issuing a penalty.

3. By October 2012, Google's would only tolerate 50% spammy links before a penalty.

That 50% figure was TWO YEARS ago (at the time of writing this). How much further has Google's tolerance shifted? How low will this percentage go? That's anybody's guess, but I have personally stopped all keyword-focused anchor text links to my own sites.

Do you have a site where you've done this in the past? Then you need to be careful and water down the percentage of anchor text rich links. Add in new links on authority sites, using article titles and URLs as the link text. Remove any poor links that you can, and disavow those that you cannot control.

You may be wondering what the current safe level is for keyword-rich anchor texts. I don't believe there is a safe level and it is certainly a moving target in the wrong direction. Let me go over what I think would be fairly safe limits.

I would recommend a link profile to a page on your site where:

1. NO MORE than 5% of backlinks use commercial keyword-rich anchor text. For all new links you build to your site, I'd recommend you no longer use keyword phrases in anchor text. Use the page title (or site title) for the page you link to, or the naked URL of that page. Rely on strong on-page factors to tell Google what the page is about, and internal linking to using keyword-rich anchor text; because this type of link IS natural (see earlier discussion about Wikipedia)

2. The other 95% of anchor text should be made up of things like the page URL, the page title, the opening H1 header text, and words that are irrelevant to the topic of the article, like "click here", "read this", "read more", "this site", "this blog", "here", etc. The most natural anchor texts to use for any link to

a page on your site are the page title and URL. Those are the ones I recommend you use the most.

What about existing keyword rich backlinks?

My suggestion if you have a lot of keyword-rich anchor text links to your site is as follows:

1. Try to change the anchor text from keywords to page titles/URLs or site name.

2. For backlinks on poor quality websites, remove the links altogether. If you cannot get the link removed, consider disavowing the link if it is on a poor quality site.

3. Build more quality backlinks on authority sites related to your niche. Use page title, site name or bare URL as the anchor text. By building better links to your site, it is possible that you can over-power the poorer links. This is something I would not have said 6 months ago, but something seems to have changed.

In October 2014, MicrositeMasters.com published a report in the aftermath of Penguin 3.0. The findings of their report were interesting, and actually give webmasters a little more hope.

2 Key points include:

1. Penguin 3.0 seems to be targeting sites that do not have enough good links.

2. Penguin 3.0 does not seem to be punishing sites for bad links, but is instead "erasing" the value of bad links.

Are Google making a U-Turn on penalizing pages with bad backlinks? This would be a major change compared to earlier Penguin updates that actively did penalize sites for bad backlinks.

One clue may come from something Matt Cutts said in the summer of 2014. When asked about negative SEO, Matt confirmed that Google was aware of it, and that the **Payday Loan 2.0** update would close some of the loopholes people were using for negative SEO. Does this mean that instead of penalizing for bad backlinks, Google are just ignoring them, making them ineffective for ranking? That would certainly backup the report on MicrositeMasters.

You can read their full report here:

http://www.micrositemasters.com/blog/penguin-3-0-analysis-what-got-hurt-what-didnt-and-3-things-you-need-to-know-to-remain-relevant/

I still don't recommend keyword rich anchor text backlinks from other websites, but this report may suggest we can stop worrying so much about existing poor quality links. Just overpower bad links with good links.

Of course, if you have thousands or even hundreds of thousands of poor backlinks to your site, the disavow tool may be needed. In some cases, moving your site to a new domain may be the only option, but you'll then need to start building your site authority from scratch again, so that really is a last, last resort.

Ranking for a main keyword phrase?

The old way we did SEO was to find popular search phrases and build pages around those phrases, optimizing the page and backlinks for the perfect ranking boost. With SEO of old, we could choose what phrases we wanted to rank for, and go after those phrases.

This strategy no longer works. As we've seen, Penguin penalizes if it thinks you've over-optimized on-page or off-page factors for a page. With the recent algorithm updates, it is now very hard to safely optimize a page for a specific term.

You can see this if you do a Google search. A lot of the pages that rank for any given term do not contain that term in the title. Some don't even include it on the page.

For example, if I search Google for the term **honey bees dying**, only 4 pages in the top 100 of Google include that exact phrase in the title. Most don't even include that phrase in the web page. The reason these pages are ranked highly is not because of the keyword phrases on the page, it's because those pages are themed around the topic of "honey bees dying", so include the words and phrases that Google knows should be on those pages. We covered all of this in the section on writing content around a theme, but it's good to mention it again to emphasize the importance.

If you want to rank for a specific phrase, this is the method I use:

1. Find theme words used on pages that rank in the top 10 at Google.

2. Write an "epic" post on the topic and theme it with the relevant niche vocabulary. Make sure the page is unique and adds additional value to the other pages in the top 10. In other words, make sure it deserves to be in the top 10.

3. Get backlinks from other authority sites in the niche, using my page title as the link text.

4. Use internal linking to my new page with a variety of link text, including the one I am targeting.

That's it; my 4 step process for ranking a page for a specific keyword phrase. The benefit of this strategy is that you can also rank for hundreds of other long-tail keyword phrases.

Backlinking from now on?

Google seem to be paying less attention to inbound anchor text and more attention to the topic of the page linking to yours.

For example, if your page is on "Health benefits of curcumin" and you got a link from a page about curcumin or turmeric, then that link would be a valuable one, irrespective of the anchor text used to link to your page.

With that in mind, I'd suggest trying to make your links look as authoritative as possible. Think how academic literature links to another article. They'll use the title of the other article or the bare URL. They might also use the journal name and edition to help find the document. If you were writing a guest post for another website with the intention of linking back to your site, instead of doing this:

Curcumin has shown remarkable anti-cancer properties not only in stripping the cancer cells defenses to make them more visible to the body's natural immune system, but also in cell apoptosis.

.. where **anti-cancer properties** is one of the phrases you want to rank for and links to your site. Do something like this instead:

Curcumin has shown remarkable anti-cancer properties not only in stripping the cancer cells defenses to make them more visible to the body's natural immune system, but in an article "Curcumin initiates cancer cells death", the author describes experimental results showing cell apoptosis occurring.

Do you see how natural this looks to a visitor? This looks like a recommendation to read more information on the topic. It looks like something to help the visitor rather than just something used to score points from a search engine? This type of link looks more authoritative, more natural to Google, AND it will be extremely valuable to your site.

If you are submitting articles to other sites for backlinking, then I'd recommend:

1. In-context links like the one above, where the link uses the article title (or URL) and the reader is in no doubt what the destination page is about.
2. A link to a URL or homepage in a resource box, though again, don't use keyword phrases as the anchor text. Use the URL, the domain name or the title of the page you are linking to.

With Penguin, we actually need fewer backlinks to rank well, but they need to be from relevant, quality web pages. Google is giving MORE weight to quality links than it used to.

OK, so where can you look for backlinks?

The Best Backlinks

The very best backlinks you can get to your site are the ones you do not create. These are backlinks from other sites, where you did not request the link, nor do you have any say in the anchor text that is used in the link. They are also the most difficult to get.

The **ideal backlinks** to your site would have the following properties:

1. Link is on a high authority site.

2. Page containing the link is related to the page it links to.

3. The page containing the link is a high quality page, with high quality content.

4. The link is in the body of the article (contextual).

5. The link uses your page title for the anchor text.

6. There are very few outbound links (to other websites) on the page.

7. The page your link appears on has a lot of human interaction (social shares, comments, etc).

8. YOU do not control the backlink.

These types of backlink are the Holy Grail of backlinks. They are very difficult to get, but are fantastic for boosting your ranking. I would prefer 4 or 5 links like this than a thousand so-so links.

So what is the best way to get quality inbound links?

The best chance you have of getting those Holy Grail backlinks is to....

... Develop Epic Content that acts as "Link Bait".

Develop content that your visitors love and want to share with others (via their social media channels). Develop content on your site that other site owners will want to link to.

When other people WANT to link to your content, we call that content "link bait", since it attracts links naturally.

Here are a few ideas for developing link bait for your site.

1. Infographics – these are graphical representations of complex topics. They are favourites for sharing on social channels e.g. Pinterest. They are also often re-posted on other sites. When you create and post an infographic on your site, you can include the HTML code for other webmasters to copy and paste onto their own site. This will display the infographic on their site, with a small link back to yours:

2. Scripts & tools that people will bookmark and share. Webmaster will always link to useful tools, especially if they are free. Here is one example of a tool that searches for the nutritional information of a food:

Another good example is a currency convertor script, where you can convert one currency to another. Or a time zone convertor. How about a cholesterol conversion tool, converting between the two popular units for cholesterol - mg/dl and mmol/L. Any tool that you can create (or get created for your site), that people find useful, will attract links from other websites as well as through social sharing.

3. Free downloads like software or PDFs that people find useful. If you can give these away, and people really do find them useful, your URL will be shared with their friends on forums they frequent and through their social media channels.

4. Posts that include "lists". People love to share lists on forums, in comments on other blogs and via their social channels. For example, "Top 10 Wordpress Plugins" on a site about building websites would be very interesting to people interested in building a Wordpress site. A post like this would get a lot of social shares, plus other sites will link to it. A tip here is to contact the authors of the plugins you recommend, and tell them that they made your top 10 list. Many will link to your post from their site, to prove to their visitors how useful their plugin is.

5. Controversial posts are always popular. When people are controversial, they usually evoke a strong response. I cannot tell you how to be controversial in your own niche, but I would just say, make your controversy factual. Making something up just to be controversial won't work and it will just annoy your visitors.

A while ago there was lots of information coming out about how good intermittent fasting was for losing weight, and health in general. Everyone was jumping on the bandwagon. One website went against the grain with a headline, something like "Intermittent fasting bad for women". It caused quite a stir. The important point about this controversy was that it was factual. The article went on to explain that certain types of women developed problems during intermittent fasting (especially those with low body fat). This controversy resulted in a lot of natural backlinks as it was discussed on blogs and forums, plus a lot of traffic.

6. Include a forum – For example, if you had a website on "Husky dogs", then a forum would attract Husky owners, who would then recommend your site to their friends and through their social channels. Building user participation through a forum on your site is a great way to attract natural links. Anyone member of your forum becomes a potential link builder for you when they are on other sites or talking to friends. Forums are very easy to add to a site using a script (check out vBulletin.com), but as a downside they do take a lot of work to maintain.

7. Interviews – Interview an expert in your niche, and use that interview to attract inbound links to your site. You needn't buy expensive equipment or software for an interview. A cheap headset and Skype is all you need.

If it is an audio only interview, post the audio on your site with a transcript of the interview. The transcript will work as search engine bait, but a lot of visitors actually prefer to read this type of thing rather than listen to it. Audio interviews can also be uploaded to audio sharing sites. Search Google for **audio upload** and look for opportunities where you can create a backlink to your site. You can create a very natural backlink on this type of audio sharing site by saying something like "Prefer a transcript? Read the full interview on ...." and link directly to your transcript page using the title of that page as anchor text.

If the interview is a video, upload the video to Youtube, plus maybe Vimeo and Dailymotion. Create a post on your own site and embed the Youtube video. Include the transcript of the video (for the same reasons as above) on your site. In the YouTube description of the video, add the URL where people can "read the transcript".

Finally, don't forget to tell the interviewee the page URL where the interview is posted on your site. They will likely link to it and possibly tell their own visitors/mailing list about the interview. It's a great way of attracting a powerful backlink from an authority site in your niche. Attracted links are links you have no control over, and remember. These are the most powerful and natural links a website can get. They will prove your site's worth to the search engines.

I'd choose one link attained in this manner over 1000 links from traditional backlinking methods.

Broken Link Building

Before we move on to look at the more traditional methods of building links, there is one form of link building that works really well. It's called broken link building, and essentially means that you look for broken links (related to your own site) on other websites and then contact the owner to tell them, offering your own link as a replacement.

As an example, let's consider a website on health and nutrition. If I owned that site, I'd go out looking for websites that have broken links to any article on health or nutrition. Let's say I find a page about the importance of vitamin A for good eye health, but one of the links on that page goes to a 404 not found error. I would contact the webmaster of the nutrition site, telling them that the link went to a 404, and tell them I have a page on the same topic if they needed a good source to link to. Offer them your URL.

The advantage of this type of link is that it is often on an aged page, possibly on an authority site. A backlink from this type of site would be a good one, added by the other webmaster and giving you no control over the link text.

So how do you go about finding broken links on related pages?

Well, there are a number of tricks we can use.

The first is to search Google for resource/links pages in our niche, using a "footprint". Here are a few that work well:

"KEYWORD links"

"KEYWORD resources"

"KEYWORD web links"

 inurl:links "KEYWORD"

Swap out KEYWORD for a phrase that is related to your niche / webpage.

That last one is an interesting search phrase, as it looks for webpages that include the word "links" in the URL, and are about your keyword. Here is an example search for that "footprint".

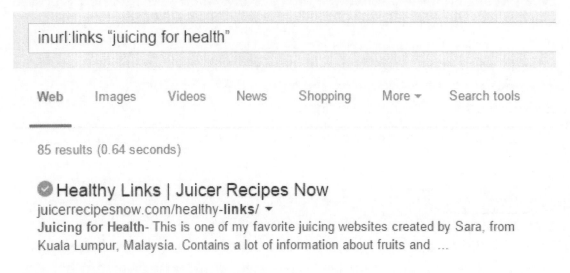

inurl:links "juicing for health"

Web   Images   Videos   News   Shopping   More ▾   Search tools

85 results (0.64 seconds)

Healthy Links | Juicer Recipes Now
juicerrecipesnow.com/healthy-**links**/ ▾
Juicing for Health- This is one of my favorite juicing websites created by Sara, from Kuala Lumpur, Malaysia. Contains a lot of information about fruits and ...

LINKS - JUicing for health
cat125juicing.weebly.com/**links**.html
JUicing for health · JUICING · Purchasing A Juicer · PRODUCE NUTRITION · RED · ORANGE/YELLOW · GREEN · BLUE/PURPLE · WHITE · Recipies · FAQ ...

See how the top 2 results are clearly links pages about "juicing for health"?

Using footprints like this offers the quickest way of finding broken link opportunities. Find the links pages and then check them to see if any links are broken.

 Before you think you need to go through every link manually, clicking on them to check for a broken link, let me tell you about a free Google Chrome extension called **Check My Links**. Search the Google Chrome store for the plugin and install it.

Once installed, you'll have a button in the toolbar for the extension. Visit a page you want to check for broken links, and click the extension button. You'll get a badge in the top right of the screen, telling you a breakdown of the links on the page:

I can see from this badge that 3 links are broken. Scrolling down the page, the links are colour coded:

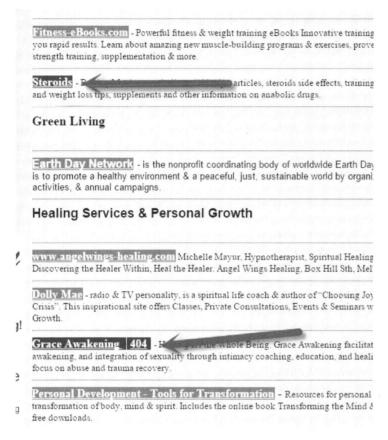

See how you can easily spot the broken links? If I had a good page on steroids, I'd be writing to this webmaster about swapping out that first link with my own.

But what if my health site did not have a page on steroids?

Simple. I'd create one.

I'd probably head off to the Way Back Machine (http://archive.org/web/) to check out the page that is currently used in that link. This free service will show you what a page looked like in the past.

Although that steroid page no longer exists, the Way Back Machine keeps cached copies of most pages. Here is the steroid page as it was on 13th April 2012:

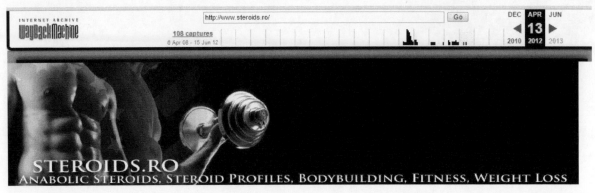

That will give me some ideas for my own steroid page before I contact the webmaster about the broken link.

At the end of the day, if that webmasters ignores me, or just deletes the broken link without using mine, I still have a great new piece of content for my own site.

The easiest broken backlinks to find are on this type of resource page since these are the types of pages webmasters typically link out to a number of external sites.

I know a lot of SEOs will tell you that links on resource pages are a waste of time, but that simply is not true. Start judging ALL backlink opportunities by the quality of the page your link would appear on.

1. Is the page good quality?

2. Does the page only link to sites within a very narrow niche topic?

3. Does the page only link to quality sites?

4. Is the page genuinely useful to visitors to that site?

5. Is that page found on a quality website?

If these guidelines apply, then the page is a good one for a backlink.

Broken backlink building is a great way to get quality backlinks on aged, authority pages in your niche.... if you can find them.

The methods mentioned above are my favourite methods of backlinking. However, this chapter would not be complete without looking at the fall-back options.

Traditional backlinking sources

Quality backlinks are difficult to get, so it's a good idea to have a plan of attack with any new link building campaign you start. I like to create one piece of content, then convert it to other formats. In other words, I create "re-purposed backlinking content" from a single article.

For example, I can create an article on a relevant topic and from that one article create:

1. A text based article for submission to another site.

2. A PDF version for submission to PDF sharing sites.

3. A slideshow presentation of the main points of the article, and upload to sites like Slideshare.net.

4. An infographic of the main points.

5. A video using the contents of the article. This can be the slideshow presentation with a voice-over. Alternatively you could use software like Easy Sketch pro to create a "whiteboard video" of the main points.

http://ezseonews.com/review/easy-sketch-pro-2-review/

From doing one piece of research you now have several different media types to use for backlinks. Let's look at the types of places you can submit these documents for backlinks.

NOTE: What follows are the typical backlink sources recommended by most SEO courses and books. Use these with caution, and I really do recommend you ignore the popular advice to use keyword rich anchor text in your backlinks. Stick with page title, site name or bare URL, and try to insert it so that it looks natural.

Article Directories

This is a strange one because some experts believe that article marketing no longer works. I personally believe that it does still work, but, it's nowhere near as effective as it used to be. Oh, and there is one more thing. Don't submit the same article to lots of article directories. A far more productive approach is to pick maybe 10 quality directories (niche specific directories are the best) and submit a unique article to each one.

I know a lot of people are tempted to write an article and use a spinner to generate 100s of unique versions to use for article marketing. Don't. Unique is not just about the words on the page, but the information in the article. A spun article is not only spam, it's also duplicate content in the eyes of Google.

OK, I hear what you are saying. This means you have to write 10 unique articles. Yes, it does, but if you want to be completely "white hat" about this, and build your authority in a way Google cannot object to, then that is what you need to do. This really is the only safe way of doing article marketing.

When adding a backlink to your site, do not simply hyperlink a relevant keyword phrase in the article. Remember Google's webmaster guidelines?

- Links with optimized anchor text in articles or press releases distributed on other sites. For example:
  There are many wedding rings on the market. If you want to have a wedding, you will have to pick the best ring. You will also need to buy flowers and a wedding dress.

Backlinks you create when article marketing should be from an author bio box at the end of your article. I'd recommend you only link to your homepage from these bio boxes, and only by using your site name or site URL as the anchor text. Don't link to an internal page from this type of backlink, and don't link using the homepage title. Stick to the site name or URL.

If you really want to get a backlink into the body of your article, go back and look at the example I gave you in the "Backlinking from now on" section to see how you can naturally use links in the body of the article. However, if you do this, do not link to the same site in the author bio box.

For the amount of effort it takes, I'd actually recommend you don't use article marketing as a strategy. Write the content, and look for guest posting opportunities on relevant sites. We'll look at guest posting later.

Forum participation

In the past, forums have been heavily spammed by webmasters looking for links. There are two obvious ways to get links from a forum. The first way is by using your forum profile, which usually has a field to enter your website URL. This backlink is typically called a forum profile link. Automated software exists that can create thousands of forum profile links automatically.

It seems obvious to me that Google can spot this type of linking very easily. Imagine a website gaining 5000 forum profile backlinks in a matter of days!

Think about the page this link will sit on. Does it meet any of the requirements for a quality page? In most cases no. It might be OK if you create a wonderful profile page with lots of content, but never create forum profiles simply for backlinks, and never use automated software! Abusing forum profile links is a quick way to get penalized in Google.

When it comes to forums, the best way to get good backlinks is to get involved in the forum and help people. Before entering a new niche, I recommend you even scout out 2 or 3 forums that allow backlinks in forum signatures, and join them. As you build your site, pop into these forums and start contributing. By the time your site is ready, you can insert your URL into your forum signature and get instant backlinks, as well as traffic from the forum visitors.

When you register with the forum, make sure you use your website email address with an attached Gravatar image (check out https://en.gravatar.com/). The image should be a photograph of yourself; the same one you use on your site. This image will then appear next to your posts in the forum. People will see your posts on different forums and start to recognize you as that "expert" they've seen before. They will start to click through to your site when they see you helping others. It's natural curiosity to want to find out more about people you see every day.

On your website they will see your picture again and this further reinforces your perceived authority. The more they see your photo and read your contributions on these forums, the more they will recognize and respect you as an authority. This is a great way to build authority and it's nothing to do with the backlinks you can get from the forums, though these are useful as well.

Imagine how high your perceived authority will be when a visitor goes to several sites (in your niche) and sees you on all of them, answering questions and providing valuable information.

YouTube & other video sites

Creating videos that offer valuable information in your niche is a great way to increase authority and "social proof" (especially if your photo or brand image appears in the video). Videos that you create do not need to be 10 or 15 minute long, you can easily create short two or three minute videos discussing short issues in your niche. Video descriptions can be quite long, and can **include a link back to your site**. If there is a relevant internal page on your site that makes the most sense to link to, do that, otherwise just link to your homepage. At the end of this book there is a bonus chapter on YouTube optimization.

YouTube allows you to create a video channel, which lists all of your videos. Your YouTube profile can even have a link back to your site, and other sites that are part of your network (Twitter, Facebook, Google+).   If someone likes one your videos, they can check out your channel to see what other videos you've created. They may even follow you on social media, or visit your website.

There are a lot of other video sharing sites as well, which will also allow you to have a profile page. Try to use the same photo that you have on your site, and that you are using for your Gravatar. We are trying to build up the recognition factor here so that people can automatically recognize you and think "Oh yes I remember this expert ..."

Twitter

Again we can use twitter to include a brand photo and link back to our main site. As we add tweets, your photo is sent through the system and ends up again in front of people that have subscribed to your twitter feed. Even if you don't have a lot of followers, your twitter page will have links back to your main site, which adds further authority to your persona.

There are a number of WordPress plugins available which automatically send a tweet for each new post published on your site. I wouldn't rely totally on this plug-in for Twitter "content", because it's important to tweet interesting information you find on a day-to-day basis on other websites. A Twitter account that only sends tweets with links to your own site, is a spammy Twitter account.

Facebook page

Another way that you can increase your authority is by setting up a Facebook page for your site or your business.

Again there are WordPress plugins that can automatically post to your Facebook page whenever you add new content to your site.

Facebook only allow you to have a single Facebook account, and one of the biggest concerns I hear from my students is that they don't want friends and/or family to be aware of their business posts on Facebook.

Don't worry. If you set up a Facebook page for your website, it is totally separate from your personal profile. You can post specifically to your website page, and none of your friends or followers will even know that page exists. You can have multiple pages promoting different websites or product. When you login to Facebook, you will see links to your pages, but your followers will not.

Web 2.0 "Blogs"

There are a number of websites that allow you to set up blogs on their domain. Examples include WordPress.com, Blogger.com (owned by Google), Tumblr.com, and LiveJournal etc. You simply go to the site, sign up, and begin posting to your new blog.

As you add more and more content to these blogs, they become more and more powerful (especially if you build backlinks to these blogs).

Since you add the blog content yourself, you can insert links into that content, but don't overdo it. These blogs should add value and be high quality, just like every other type of backlink we are looking to build. I recommend you create small blogs with 5 to 10 pages of great content related to your main site. Then add a single backlink to your main site, from the homepage of the mini-site. That's right. Each of these mini-sites will contain just ONE link to your main site. Make your link the only external link on the homepage. On the other pages in the mini-site, link out naturally to authority sites in your niche. Use different types of content and make the mini-site look natural.

Try to get a few backlinks to each of the mini-sites you build. But again, make sure the backlinks are high quality.

RSS feeds

If you use WordPress to build your site, then you have an RSS feed for your site. An RSS feed contains all of the most recent posts. You define how many posts show in the feed within the WordPress Dashboard.

You can find the feed by adding "/feed" to the end of your URL (without the quotes obviously).

For example:

http://ezseonews.com/feed/

Once you have your feed URL, you can submit that feed to a number of different RSS Feed websites.

Every time you add new content to your site, the feed is updated, and you get a link back to the new content.

I don't believe that this type of link helps too much with ranking of pages, especially as posts will slide off the bottom of the feed eventually, but it does help to get new content indexed quickly.

I would recommend submitting your feed to only two or three of the highest authority RSS directories that you can find.

I'd also recommend that you set up your feed to only display excerpts (and a maximum of 10 posts). This should keep you safe from spammers who will try to scrape your content by stripping the posts from your feed. Having only 10 posts in the feed is more of a safety precaution as we don't want the last 100 posts hyperlinked on 3 different RSS feed directory sites. This would look like we're trying to manipulate rankings.

Site directories

Getting your site listed in directories is one of the oldest forms of backlinking. These days, directory listings are not as powerful as they used to be, and there are a number of directories you absolutely should not submit your site to (any low quality, or niche directories unrelated to your own site).

There are software programs that can submit your site to multiple directories, but I would suggest you save your money and just handpick the most relevant ones (particularly the specialist niche directories that match your chosen niche), and then submit by hand. More is NOT better. Always look for fewer quality submissions where the submission site is a close match to your own. For example, if you have a Paleo diet site, look for directories that specialise in nutrition.

Guest blogging

Guest Blogging is a powerful way to get high quality links back to your site. It's kind of like *Article Marketing 2.0* where you submit articles to sites that accept "guest posts".

The big difference between guest posting and article directories is that guest blogs can be higher quality and much more related to your own niche. For example, you could find a lot of health-related blogs that would accept health related articles from you, but it would be harder to find article directories that were specifically health related.

Guest posting works like this:

There are sites out there that are looking for people to write content for them. You write a piece of content and submit it to these sites. If they like your article, they will post it on their website.

When you post your article, you include a resource box that can include links back to your website (or a link in the body of your article). You do need to check the terms and conditions of the sites you are writing for to see whether it's possible to include links within the body of the article. If you can, do that, but make your links look authoritative, like we discussed earlier. Remember, this:

> Curcumin has shown remarkable <u>anti-cancer properties</u> not only in stripping the cancer cells defenses to make them more visible to the body's natural immune system, but also in cell apoptosis.

That looks a lot more spammy than this:

Curcumin has shown remarkable anti-cancer properties not only in stripping the cancer cells defenses to make them more visible to the body's natural immune system, but in an article "Curcumin initiates cancer cells death", the author describes experimental results showing cell apoptosis occurring.

The second one is also more Google friendly, as it is not using keyword anchor text. Instead it uses the title of the article being linked to, like a real reference.

Finding Guest Blogs

You can easily find sites that will accept your work by doing a Google search for:

"write for us" + KEYWORD

Where KEYWORD is your main niche word or phrase.

e.g. "write for us" + health

This will return all of the websites that have the phrase "Write for Us" and are related to the health industry. Here are the top few Google results for that term:

86. The **Health** Care Blog
thehealthcareblog.com/
3 hours ago – The Business of **Health** Care ... Last year was a banner year for digital **health**, as the market saw significant growth in ..... WRITE FOR US ...

SEOquake | PR: 6 ←

87. **Write for Us** | Help & Info | Her.meneutics
www.christianitytoday.com/women/help/about-us/**write-for-us**.html
Home > Help & Info > **Write for Us** ... parenting, and celibacy, pop culture, **health** and body image, raising girls, and women in the church and parachurch.

SEOquake | PR: 5 ←

NOTE: PageRank data is being displayed in the SERPs using a free browser plugin called SEO Quake. This is available for Firefox, Chrome, Opera and Safari.

With guest blogging, you can pretty much guarantee getting your content onto high PR websites.

These sites can have a lot of authority in the eyes of Google and are therefore excellent places to get your content published. However, there are other benefits too.

Not only do you get backlinks from an authority site, but you'll also get to post your picture and site URL, which only further boosts your own personal authority in the niche. Each article that gets accepted is exposed to a new audience – one that your own site probably never gets. In this way, guest blogging is a great method to "piggy back" on other peoples traffic.

PDF distribution

PDF files (that can contain links to your website) can be distributed to a number of websites. Again, each site you distribute the PDF to can include your profile picture and link back to your site. To create PDFs, you can use existing content or simply write new content for the PDF file.

Microsoft Word or the free OpenOffice suite, both have built in features to convert text documents into PDF format.

One of the best-known examples of a site that you can upload PDF documents to is:

http://www.scribd.com/

You can find a lot of websites that accept PDF submissions by searching Google for "submit ebooks" or "submit PDF".

Again, like everything else, look for quality sites and think less about quantity.

Blog Commenting

Blog commenting is easy. Go to a webpage related to your own, and leave a comment with a link back to your own site.

Blog commenting has been heavily abused, and gets a lot of bad press. However, I've done tests recently and found that they do still work if done properly. They won't give you a massive boost in rankings, but they will diversify your backlink profile.

For the perfect blog comment, look for a quality site that allows comments, is in your niche, and preferably does not use the nofollow attribute on comment links. If it does use nofollow, don't let that put you off. Nofollow links may not count for much, but they are part of a natural link profile.

To create a comment:

1. Read the article you are commenting on. Read other people's comments too.

2. Add a comment that interacts with the original author, or another commenter. The comment should add to the conversation on that page. Add something that the webmaster will want to approve.

3. When adding a comment, you'll have fields for name and website. If there is no website field, don't waste time leaving a comment. In the name field, add your real name (or the penname you use on your site), either first or full name is fine. Never add a keyword phrase in the name field. In the URL field, enter your website homepage URL.

4. Be aware that many webmasters delete comments with URLs in the body. Never add links to the body of your comment, unless there is a really good reason for doing so (ie answering someone's question).

Backlink Velocity

The speed at which you create backlinks to a site can raise a red flag with Google.

If you have a site that gets 10 visitors a day, does it make sense that the site has 50 backlinks to it? Not if those backlinks were all obtained naturally (other people independently linking to your site because of the great content).

I would recommend starting off very slowly with any new site, and it is important that the backlink profile to your site is diverse! This means lots of different types of backlinks from a wide range of IP addresses.

My primary goal for any new site is to create **epic** content that will attract links, and share it with social media channels in the hope it becomes popular and is shared around.

After creating several pieces of quality content in an attempt to attract links, I'll turn my attention to creating a few links. First up, I'll look for broken link opportunities and try to get a few from sites related to my niche. Once I've exhausted those, I'll look at using my "re-purposed" backlink content to get backlinks from some of those other sources we mentioned above.

However, do it slowly. A link or two every week is perfect for a new site. Once your visitors pick up, you can go a little faster, but in 2015, quality of backlinks is far more important than quantity. In fact, quantity will only work against you in the long-run if those links are low quality.

When to stop backlinking

If you have the link-bait style content we discussed at the beginning of this section, then your pages will attract links naturally, and you should concentrate on adding new, high quality content to keep your visitors happy and attract new links.

If you don't have content that naturally attracts links, you will need to going out looking for backlinks, and I'd recommend you do so on a continuous basis.

As discussed earlier, I'd recommend using the title of the page you are linking to, or its bare URL as the link text.

Avoid using keyword rich anchor text, because there is a real danger of over-optimization. Google may decide you have too many spammy links and penalize the site. If you want keyword rich anchor texts pointing to a page on your site, link to it from other pages within the site.

As we mentioned earlier, don't worry about trying to rank at the top of Google for specific keyword terms. If your page deserves to rank at the top of the SERPs for a phrase, it will have more chance of doing so if you concentrate on building tour authority over time. Remember that Google knows what your page is about. They don't need over-optimized anchor text to tell them. If they think it's worthy of #1, they'll rank it #1. If they don't, then work more on the quality/value of the content, and authority of your site/page. Also bear in mind that pages that are optimized for a keyword phrase (especially commercial keyword phrases) rarely rank well for that phrase.

Backlinks to backlinks

Whenever you build a site you should be tracking a lot of information. One of the most important things to track is the backlinks pointing to your site.

Majestic SEO is a good free tool to do just this.

Once you have set up Majestic SEO, wait for the data to start coming in.

You will get a list of all the backlinks pointing to your site. Download the list (Majestic allows you to download the list as a spreadsheet) and check them to make sure that the backlinks still exist. Delete any links that no longer exist so you only end up with a list of web pages that actively link to your site.

Work your way through the list, and create backlinks to each of these backlinks.

You can use any method of backlinking you want but I would recommend you only point quality links at these backlinks. This obviously means more work on your behalf, but I'll explain why it's important a little later. The idea is to make each page linking to your page stronger, and therefore able to pass more link juice to your site.

Here it is as a diagram:

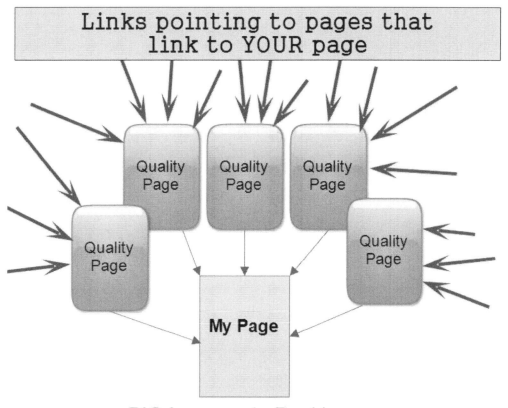

In my opinion, many webmasters go wrong with this type of backlinks to backlink strategy. They often tend not worry about the quality of the backlinks to their backlinks. Instead they blast thousands of profile links, social bookmarks, spun articles, etc. at their main backlinks in an attempt to boost them.

Most webmasters that use this strategy assume that their site is safe, since these poor quality spammy links DO NOT point at their own site, but at the backlinks to their site (these sites that hold our backlinks are often referred to as buffer sites). They assume that these buffer sites provide a type of immunity against a penalty.

However..... Google hates linking schemes, and pyramid systems like this are no exception. Is it too farfetched to think that the negative SEO we saw earlier could render this type of link pyramid not only useless, but harmful to your site? In the diagram above, if those links to your backlinks are good quality, you have nothing to worry about. However, what if those links pointing at your backlinks are low quality, spammy links? Let's re-draw that diagram.

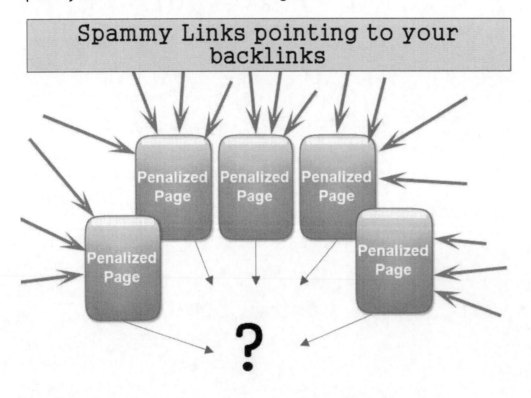

Now, instead of quality links pointing at the backlinks we have poor quality, spammy links, which in turn, penalize the pages that hold your backlinks. What happens now when those pages link to your site?

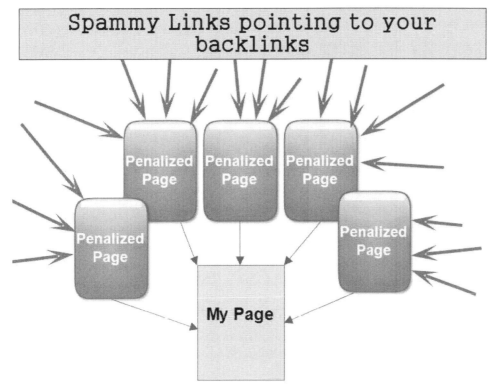

Page gets a penalty and loses rankings

The penalty would be passed down the pyramid, and your page penalized.

When Google decided to pass negative ranking factors through links (allowing negative SEO to work), it allowed penalties to pass down pyramid linking schemes; removing any immunity that was previously available through buffer sites.

A few years ago, everyone assumed that negative SEO was impossible. That is, if you wanted to take out your competition by pointing a lot of poor links at their site, it wouldn't work. Google even told us it wouldn't work. However, today we know this is no longer true. The truth is, poor quality inbound links can hurt a webpage.

It makes sense though, doesn't it? I mean *if* Google introduced a system where poor links pass on a negative ranking factor, then they would be wasting a massive opportunity to wipe out a lot of spammers if they didn't allow these penalties to trickle down the link pyramids.

So how do we stop someone else building spammy links to our website in an attempt to get our site penalized? Well the simple answer is that we cannot.

You may remember a recent report I mentioned earlier by the MicrositeMasters.com which suggested bad links were losing their ability to negatively affect a site rankings. If this is true, we can stop worrying so much about negative SEO and just concentrate on building high quality links.   However just to make sure, I'd recommend you take a look at the Disavow tool.   This is a tool Google gave us to help fight back against negative SEO. In giving us this tool, Google effectively said that all links to our website, good or bad, are our sole responsibility.

The Disavow Tool - how to fix bad links to your site

Several years ago, webmasters were not held responsible for the links pointing to their own sites. Negative SEO just did not work, and Google themselves told us that bad links could not hurt a site's rankings.

In the last year or two, things changed. Google changed the rules so that bad backlinks could hurt page (and site) rankings. However, because of the whole negative SEO angle, Google needed to provide a system to make webmasters truly accountable for the links to their sites, whether they had created them or not. In other words, if a website became the target of a negative SEO campaign, Google wanted the webmaster to fix it. The Disavow tool was born.

The Disavow tool allows webmasters to report bad links pointing at their sites, in the hope that Google will not count them as part of that site's backlink profile.

Therefore, if someone points a lot of spammy links at your site to try to get your site penalized, you now have a tool that you can use to tell Google about those links, and hopefully get them devalued to the point where they don't contribute to your rankings.

Before we look at the Disavow tool, let me just state something. Just because we can report bad links to Google, does not mean Google will listen or take action. Google has said that webmaster should use the Disavow tool as a last resort. The first step should always be to contact webmasters who are linking to you and ask for links to be removed. If those webmasters refuse to remove links, or ignore your requests, then that is what the Disavow tool is for.

I should also mention that if Google do disavow links, it can take some time. One of my sites was the victim of negative SEO, and after disavowing those bad links, it took around 6 months for the site to recover. I recommend you constantly monitor the backlinks to your site (Google Webmaster Tools will show you the recent backlinks it has found) and disavow spammy links as you find them.

Checking your link profile & creating a disavow file

The first step in using the Disavow tool is to find the links that point to your site and evaluate them. You need to identify the links that may be causing your site harm. These links include:

1. Those on pages with scraped content.
2. Links on pages with spun content.
3. Links on pages with very poor/limited content (in terms of language, spelling, grammar, etc).
4. Links on sites that have been penalised in Google.
5. Links on irrelevant sites, or sites with dubious content.
6. Site-wide links that appear on all of the pages of a linking website.
7. Any link that you would not want Google to manually inspect.

Fortunately, Google Webmaster Tools provides us with an easy way to do a link audit. You need a free Webmaster Tools account for this with your site linked to that account.

Assuming your website is linked to your Webmaster Tools account, Google will list the backlinks to your site. It can take a while for these backlinks to start being reported, so link up your site as soon as possible

Log in to Webmaster Tools and click on the site you want to inspect.

Now in the menu on the left, select **Links to You Site** from the **Search Traffic** menu.

On the right, you'll see a list of links to your site:

Links to Your Site

Total links
12,787

Who links the most

limesurvey.org	782
blogspot.com	255
topalternate.com	159
similarpages.com	155
youtube.com	145

More »

Google only shows you a few by default, but if you look at the bottom of the list, you'll see a link to **More**.

Click it.

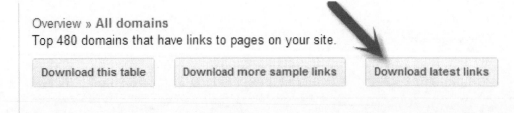

Overview » **All domains**
Top 480 domains that have links to pages on your site.

Download this table   Download more sample links   Download latest links

You now have a button to **Download latest links**. Clicking this button will allow you to choose the format of the download.

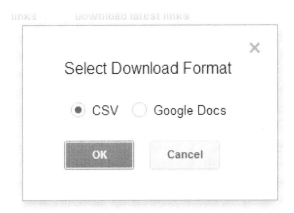

The CSV format will download a spreadsheet you can view in Excel or similar spreadsheet program. Alternatively, you can download in Google Docs format.

If you don't use Google Docs, I recommend you give it a try. Just go to **docs.google.com**

Login to Google Docs with your Gmail address and password.

If you select Google Docs from Webmaster Tools and click the OK button, the spreadsheet opens directly in Google Docs:

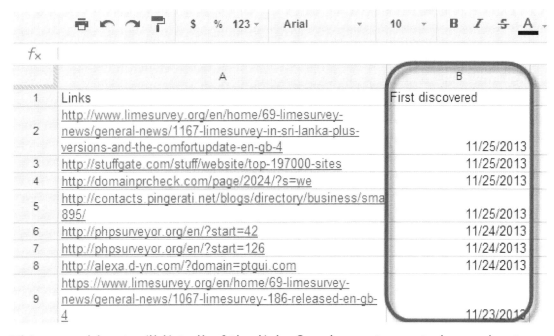

This spreadsheet will list all of the links Google wants you to know about.

Not only do you get the URL, you also get the date that the link was first discovered. This means you can check all of the links the very first time you do a link audit, and then in a month or two, you only need to check the new links that Google are reporting since your last check.

You need to work your way through the list of links, and pull out any that you really think are harming your website.

Google gives you two ways to deal with bad links. You can either report them on a link by link basis, or you can report a whole domain so any links on that domain will be disavowed. You can create a plain text file to use as your disavow list.

To disavow a single URL, just list the URLs, one on each line.

The format for reporting an entire domain is as follows:

Domain:somebaddomain.com

Google also encourages you to use comments in your disavow file. These comments can be for you, or for Google, outlining steps you have carried out to get links removed. For example, if you have tried contacting a webmaster to get links removed and they have ignored your requests, you can include that information in a comment, before listing the appropriate URLs or domain.

Comments are included by simply using the # symbol. A valid comment would be something like this:

Webmaster has ignored my request to remove these links

If you want to write more, just go onto a second line, with the # at the start. For example:

Webmaster has not replied to my emails requesting link removal

Contacted on 16/08/2013 and again on 06/09/2013

Google provide the following example as a valid disavow file:

```
# example.com removed most links, but missed these
http://spam.example.com/stuff/comments.html
http://spam.example.com/stuff/paid-links.html
# Contacted owner of shadyseo.com on 7/1/2012 to
# ask for link removal but got no response
domain:shadyseo.com
```

In their example, they want two URLs disavowed, plus all links on the shadyseo.com domain.

One you have built up your disavow file, you need to upload it to Google. One thing I recommend you do is to add the following comment to the beginning of your disavow file:

Last updated 10/10/2013

Save the file to your computer. The next time you want to do a link audit, you will know the date of your last audit and can just look at the new links since that date (remember that Google gives us the date a link was found).

Uploading the disavow file to Google is simple.

Go to this URL:

https://www.google.com/webmasters/tools/disavow-links-main

You will need to login using your Webmaster Tools login details (if you are not already logged in).

Select the website from the drop down list, and click the Disavow button:

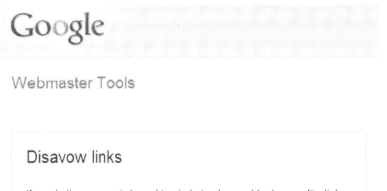

You will get a warning before you can upload the disavow file:

Disavow Links

This is an advanced feature and should only be used with caution. If used incorrectly, this feature can potentially harm your site's performance in Google's search results. We recommend that you only disavow backlinks if you believe that there are a considerable number of spammy, artificial, or low-quality links pointing to your site, and if you are confident that the links are causing issues for you.

Disavow Links

If you want to proceed, click the **Disavow Links** button.

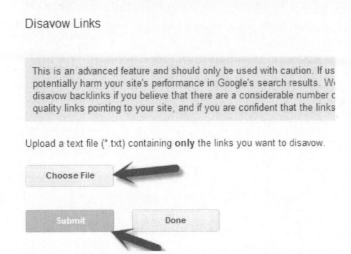

Now you have a button to **Choose File**. Click that and select your disavow text file.

Finally, click the **Submit** button to upload the file to Google.

Updating the disavow file

When you need to update the disavow file (e.g. to include more URLs or domains), simply add the new URLs and domains to the file, change the comment at the top to the current date so you can keep track, then come back to the disavow tool and re-upload your updated file. Google only keep one file per site, so the last one you upload will be the file they use for any "disavowing".

I'd recommend you do a complete link audit on your site, and then check new links every month or two. Now that you are responsible for all links to your site, you need to know who is linking to your site, and whether those links are potentially harmful to your rankings. If they are, disavow them.

I also want you to think about something else.

If there is a spammy web page linking to you, and you know that it can only be harmful to your rankings, it is possible that the site in question has more than one link to your site, even though you are not aware of them all. In cases like this, I always disavow the whole site rather than just the URLs. If the page on that site is so bad you want to disavow it, then chances are that the whole site is pretty bad.

Summary of Backlinks

Just remember these simple guidelines. When getting links:

1. Try to get links from as many different places as possible (we want IP diversity).
2. Look for quality rather than quantity. A handful of quality links will do more

for your rankings than hundreds or thousands of spammy links (which actually could get your site penalized). Look for the "Holy Grail" backlinks by creating content other people want to link to.

3. Don't use keyword rich anchor text in links you obtain from other websites. Always use your website title, URL, page URL or title of the page you are linking to as the anchor text.
4. Use internal linking to introduce keyword rich links to a page.
5. With links coming in from other websites, keep the percentage of any one anchor text to 5% or less.
6. Backlink your backlinks to make them stronger, but only backlink using high quality links. By strengthening your backlinks like this, you'll need fewer of them to compete.
7. Carry out a link audit periodically on your site, and disavow any low quality, spammy links that may be affecting your rankings.

4. What's in it for the visitor?

When somebody arrives on your website, you have a very short time to make a first impression. That first impression will decide whether they stay or go, so the first thing you need to do is make sure your site looks good. If you're using WordPress, then that's quite easy because there are a lot of very attractive WordPress designs out there.

Apart from the design, another aspect of your site which will add to that first impression is the speed at which the page loads. This needs to be as fast as possible to avoid having visitors waiting for stuff to load.

Install Google Analytics and get a Google Webmaster Tools account

These tools can give you a huge amount of information on your site and your visitors. They are also Google's way to communicate with YOU! If there is anything Google in concerned about, they'll tell you about it in your Webmaster account. They'll also notify you when your site is down or there is a WordPress upgrade (if you use WordPress).

A lot of webmasters think it's best to avoid these tools as Google will use them against you, but I disagree. Google already has all the data they need on your site, and its tools are a way of sharing that data with you.

Google's "Webmaster Tools" use to tell you how fast your site was loading and show you a graph of load times over a period of time. However, they have since retired this tool. You can now find that information in Google Analytics though.

A great alternative to checking your page load speed is to use an online tool like GTMetrix (http://gtmetrix.com/). You simply enter your page URL and GTMetrix will measure the load speed there and then, in real-time:

Report generated: Fri, Feb 22, 2013, 2:06 AM -0800

Test Server Region: Vancouver, Canada

Using: Firefox 14.0.1, Page Speed 1.12.9.1, YSlow 3.1.4

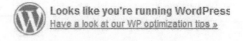

Looks like you're running WordPress
Have a look at our WP optimization tips »

Summary

Page Speed Grade: (81%)	B	YSlow Grade: (76%)	C	Page load time: 2.63s Total page size: 916KB Total number of requests: 81

Not only do they give you time in seconds for the page load, but they'll tell you which parts of your site are slowing things down, and what you can do to fix the problems.

Website stickiness

In Google Analytics, Google will tell you the average time a visitor stays on your site, as well as the bounce rate (how quickly someone bounces back to Google after reaching your site).

Bounce rate and time on site are a measure of how "Sticky" your site is.

Here is the bounce rate for one of my sites over the last month:

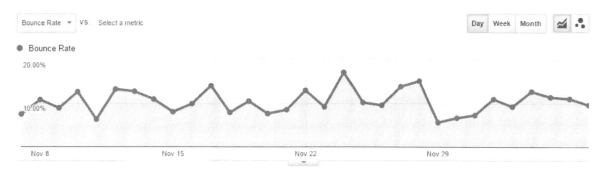

This is the average for the whole site.

You'll notice that the maximum bounce rate over the last month was under 20%, with the average being around 10%. This means that only around 10% of people visiting my site go straight back to Google after reaching the landing page. Here are the averages for this site over the last month:

The average bounce rate of 10.32% and average time on site of around 20 minutes is good. I'd say that the site was quite sticky, wouldn't you?

While that data is for the site as a whole, you can examine these metrics for individual pages to see where your site is being let down. Find the content that does not hold your visitor's attention and fix it.

The next screenshot shows the data for a number of URLs on my site.

Avg. Time on Page	En.		Bounce Rate
00:20:04 Site Avg: 00:20:04 (0.00%)		8 (98)	10.32% Site Avg: 10.32% (0.00%)
00:54:04		)	6.98%
00:05:23	19	)	31.90%
01:08:36	18	%)	4.85%
01:20:36		%)	4.93%
00:06:14		%)	10.27%
00:17:28		%)	8.18%
01:20:31		)	5.31%
01:10:07			16.00%
01:09:19		)	7.45%
00:02:48		%)	0.00%

Just look for the pages with the lowest "Avg. Time on Page" and the highest "Bounce Rate" and see if there is something you can do about those pages to improve that content and make it sticker. Any page with a high bounce rate is a clear indicator that it is not giving the visitor the "experience" they are looking for.

A lot of what follows in this chapter is already covered throughout this book, but it is nice to have all of these ideas in one place, for easier reference as you work on your site. Let's look at the key ideas to keep in mind as you work on your website.

Important aspects of a web page

You need to capture the visitor's attention and let them know what you have got for them.

In terms of articles on your website, this can mean an eye catching headline that makes them want to read more. If your visitor reads the headline and finds it interesting, they'll then read the first paragraph. The first paragraph is almost as vital as the headline itself, so you might like to try creating an opening paragraph as a summary of what your visitor will find further down the page. Tell them what goodies await further down the page.

As you write content, try to keep sentences short (20 – 25 words) as well as paragraphs – four or five sentences. People hate large blocks of text, but also hate sentences that are so long they become confusing. When you have finished your content, read it aloud. Make sure there are no parts that you have to reread to fully understand, and no parts that you hesitate over as you read them.

To make your articles easier to read, use sub-heading and bullet points. Pictures and diagrams can also help break up blocks of text, making it easier for the visitor. It's like that old adage goes; a picture is worth a thousand words.

NOTE: Use ALT tags on images, but do not keyword stuff them. Simply use an ALT tag that describes the image.

Another important point is to use colors and fonts wisely. Don't put white fonts on black background or any other combination that causes eye strain. Black font on white background is the best, and use fonts that are designed to work online like the Verdana, Trebuchet and Georgia.

If you want to see some truly shocking usage of color on the web, search Google images for the term **bad website design**.

While we're talking about content, be aware that people are a lot less patient than they used to be (http://news.bbc.co.uk/2/hi/technology/7417496.stm), so be succinct and to the point. Don't waffle just to get the number of words on the page higher.

To make your site sticky, you need to give your visitors what they want. In order to do that you need to know your visitor. Ask yourself:

- Who is it?
- What do they want?
- What answers to they need?
- What do they want to ask me?

Your homepage should guide the visitor quickly and easily to the section of your website that interests them. Your visitor should be able to find what they require swiftly and effortlessly. Needless to say a search box is essential, but that is easy with WordPress ;)

Ways to build Trust

1. A photo of yourself in a prominent position on your website. The sidebars or in the logo are a good place for this. A photo helps build trust because the visitor can see who they are interacting with.
2. If you use your photo as a Gravatar, then every time you post comments on other sites, your photo will appear. This goes back to what we were saying in

the section on building authority. How much better is it for a visitor to arrive on your site and recognize your face? This can really help towards building a high level of trust.

3. Fresh content - If people arrive at your site and see that the content is several years old, this may be enough for them to click the back button. Keep stuff like reviews up to date. If you update a review, change the timestamp of the post in WordPress to reflect the new date. If the content is "ageless" consider removing the date/time stamp from the post.

4. A clearly and visible privacy policy, terms of use and a contact page are great ways to help build trust. On your contact page you should ideally have a real address as this helps with the trust building. Again, it's a good idea to have your photo on the contact us page.

5. Create an About Us page where you can mention who you are and what your goals are for the site. On many sites, this is often one of the highest traffic pages, so don't be afraid to insert a signup box if you have a newsletter to offer.

Types of content your visitors want:

1. Answer real questions – you can find questions that people ask in your niche by looking at sites like Yahoo Answers, Quora and even Ask.com. Find real questions and create a Q&A section on your site using those questions. You can use the **site:** operator at Google to search for information on specific sites. Here is an example where I am searching Google for questions about juicing v blending at Quora.com:

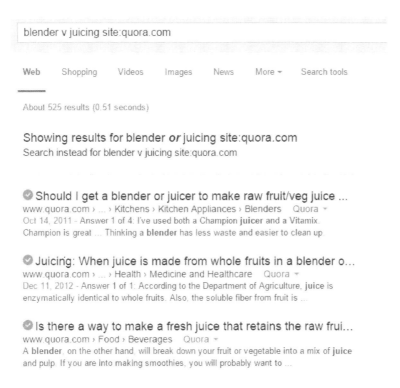

I am sure you can see how easy it is to find relevant, on-topic questions to use as the basis for website content.

2. Buyer guides – e.g. if your site is about Android Tablets, give your visitors a free PDF that tells them what they need to know when it comes to buying one. You can use that free guide to build a list if you want, by making visitors opt-in to your list before they are given the download URL.

3. Tutorials – Provide helpful tutorials for your visitors if you can think of some that are relevant to your niche.

4. Videos - Create informative, relevant videos and embed them in your web pages. Put a great title above the video to make sure your visitor clicks to watch (never have them start automatically – give your visitor the option).

Make sure the video content lives up to the title! Upload videos to Youtube.com and develop your own YouTube channel in your chosen niche. This will not only bring traffic, but also build credibility and trust. You can link to this channel from your site.

5. One type of page I usually include on my niche sites is a Terminology page. A niche has its own vocabulary as we have seen, and often people want to know what certain words or phrases mean.

When creating new content, or looking for new ideas, ask yourself this question.

"What valuable information or resources can you offer that are not available on the top 10 pages in Google?"

Make your site interactive

1. Allow Comments from visitors at the end of your articles. Invite or encourage your visitors to use the comment box. It's amazing how simple it is to say "Hey, if you've got a question or an opinion on this, leave a comment at the bottom of this post", yet a lot of people don't bother.

Darren Rowse wrote a nice article on getting your visitors to comment:

http://www.problogger.net/archives/2006/10/12/10-techniques-to-get-more-comments-on-your-blog/

A lot of webmasters turn comments off on their site because of the huge amounts of spam they receive. However, by using a good spam blocker like Akismet (commercial) or Stop Spammers (https://wordpress.org/plugins/stop-spammer-registrations-plugin/), you can eliminate 99% of all spam.

Comments allow your visitor to interact with YOU (and other commenters). If a visitor asks a question, make sure you answer it. This starts a dialogue with your target audience and builds trust and authority. Visitors see that you're actually answering questions personally. Answering questions brings visitors back to your site, especially if you have a plug-in installed that allows them to track responses to their comments.

2. By using a ratings and review plug-in (search the WordPress plugin directory for one), you can give your visitors the chance to award products their own star rating when they leave a comment.

3. Polls – Allow your visitors to express their opinion by voting. There are free polling scripts available.

4. Provide Social Media Icons after each post so that people can spread the word on your great content. There are a number of free plugins available, but I recommend you try out a few to see which one works best on your site.

5. Add a forum. This can be a lot of work because forums are often spammed heavily, but forums are a great way for people to interact with yourself and others. Several WordPress plugins are available that will add a fully functional forum on your site.

BONUS Chapter - YouTube SEO

YouTube is owned by Google. Even if you didn't know that, you might have guessed there was a close relationship by looking at how many YouTube videos rank in the top 10 of Google. YouTube videos ranked in the top 10 probably get quite good click through rates, simply because they have a thumbnail image of the video displayed in the SERPs.

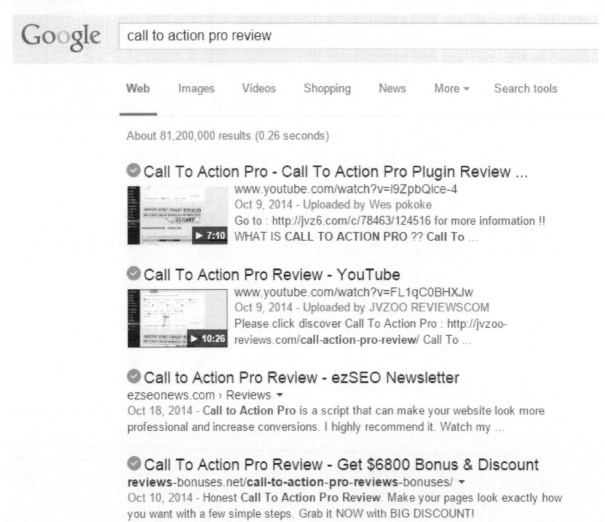

There are two videos for the above search phrases, ranked #1 and #2 on Google.

YouTube is also a major search engine in its own right, with many people using the search box on YouTube to find what they are looking for, bypassing Google completely. However, just because Google own YouTube, does not mean that the ranking algorithms on YouTube and Google are the same. Here, look at this search on YouTube for that same search phrases:

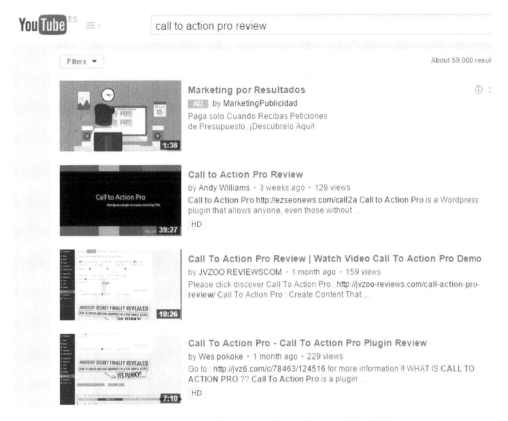

The video ranked #1 on Google is ranked #4 on YouTube.

The video ranked #2 on Google is ranked #12 on YouTube.

We've already seen that the ranking algorithm for Google is very complex, involving hundreds of different signals, both on page, and off.

YouTube's ranking is not as complex, or at least it does not appear to be.

On YouTube it is possible to rank a video using just on-page factors in less competitive niches. For example, in that screenshot above, my video is #1 (the very top video is a paid advert, so I'm not including that). If I search for that term in quotes, YouTube tells me that there are 185 videos using that exact phrase somewhere on the page. Therefore with around 185 direct competitors, I can easily rank #1.

The ease of ranking on YouTube in low competition niches has gotten some marketers excited. They reason that by finding low competition phrases with good search volume, they can rank high on YouTube and get easy traffic. Let me burst that bubble. Ranking on YouTube is great, but where you really want your video ranking is in the Google SERPs. That is where the majority of traffic will come from.

Let me give you an example.

Here is a search phrase that I found in Google Keyword Planner:

Ad group ideas	Keyword ideas		
Search terms		▼ Avg. monthly searches ?	Cor
call to action examples		∟〜 3,600	Lov

That screenshot tells me that this phrase is searched for 3,600 times a month, right?

OK, the first thing to do is see how many videos are actually optimized for that exact phrase.

A search on YouTube in quotes, tells me 338 videos use that exact phrase on the page.

An intitle:"call to action examples" search tells me that only 11 videos use that exact phrase in the title. This is often a good indicator of how many videos have been optimized for a phrase.

It's probably going to be easy to rank at the top of YouTube with just on-page factors.

If you could rank #1 in YouTube for that phrase, how much traffic would it bring?

Google Keyword Planner tells us that the phrase is searched for 116 times a day.

Well, let's go over to YouTube and see how many times the top videos ranking for that phrase have been watched:

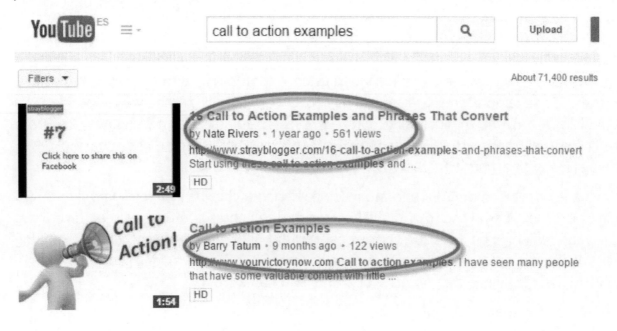

The number #1 ranked video has been watched 561 times in the 20 months since it was published. I know the YouTube screenshot says it is a year old, but if you click through to the video you can see it was published much earlier.

That means the video has had around 28 views per month.

The video in position #2 of YouTube has been seen 14 times per month.

What happened to the 3600 searches a month?

There are two problems with using search volume reported by Google Keyword Planner.

1. The search volume is for Google, not YouTube.

2. The search volume is not very accurate.

For a video on YouTube to get good traffic, it needs either a lot of search traffic ON YouTube, or the video needs to rank for the keyword phrase on Google, in the top 10 and preferably near the top.

For any search phrase, if there are videos in the top 10, that's a good sign. However, to make sure people are really using those search phrases, check how many times those videos have been watched on a monthly basis.

Before you spend time creating a video for YouTube with the sole purpose of bringing in more traffic, ask yourself "are there YouTube videos in the top 10 for this phrase, and how many views per month do those videos get?"

YouTube Video Optimization

This really is a two-part process.

1. Get the on-page factors right.

2. Build backlinks to the video from the best sources you can find.

These two steps will allow your video to rank near or at the top in YouTube, but also have a chance of ranking in Google's top 10 (assuming Google usually shows at least one video in the SERPs for that phrase).

Let's consider the on-page factors for YouTube videos.

The on-page SEO is much more like the Google SEO of old. Keywords are still King, and spamming does work. I would however, caution against creating spammy video titles or descriptions because it is only a matter of time before Google crack the whip. In fact, the YouTube results are so spammy in some niches that I am surprised Google hasn't already dealt with the problem.

OK, here is a checklist of on-page optimization you can follow to optimize your video for a specific phrase.

1. Keyword phrase in the video title. Put the phrase at the start, and try to make the title as short as possible.

2. Use your main keyword phrase in the video filename.

3. Think of the description in the same way as you would think of a short article for your site. This will give it more chance of ranking in Google. Create a well-themed description that uses the main keyword phrase in the first sentence, plus all of the important niche vocabulary further down. Include a link back to your website as a bare URL.

4. You need to add some tags to your submission. Make sure your main keyword is the first one. Include variations on that main keyword in the tags, and any other important niche vocabulary.

5. If you get comments on your videos, moderate them. Remove any spammy comments and reply to any questions you get. Engage the people that leave comments.

6. Embed the video in a page on your own website, and provide some kind of commentary (as text) to accompany the video (a video on its own is scraped content even if you created it). I often write longer articles and create a video to cover one aspect. The video then becomes a small unique part of the web page content.

7. If your videos have a lot of speech, you might consider looking into the closed caption features provided by YouTube. YouTube will try to transcribe your video automatically for you, but it's not always good, and you can download the file and correct it. If you do this, you can use the corrected transcription on your own site to accompany the video.

That's all there is to on-page optimization for YouTube videos.

However, after uploading your video, I recommend you use the social sharing buttons to share it to all of your social media channels. These will count as backlinks, albeit weak ones, but they give your video a chance to spread through social channels if it's good enough.

Things not to do with YouTube

There are a lot of services out there that promise to help you with your YouTube promotions. The popular ones offer:

1. To send visitors to your video, boosting the number of views.

2. To provide your video with a gazillion "Likes".

3. To give you subscribers to your channel.

My advice is DO NOT use any service that artificially inflates metrics of your video, even if they say they are real people. They won't be.

YouTube remains one of the safest forms of backlinks to your site, so use them for that, as well as driving traffic through links in the description. You can even monetize your YouTube videos with Adsense if you want to, so look into that if it's something that interests you. A video that goes viral with advertising on it can give you an unexpected windfall.

Where to go from here

That's it! That's my SEO guide for 2015 and beyond.

So what's next?

For anyone interested in learning my own methods for building authority sites, backlinking and SEO in general, you can join my free internet marketing newsletter.

Finally I want to wish you good luck, and I hope that you enjoyed this book.

If you did (or even if you didn't), PLEASE add a review on the Amazon website. You can find the book listing by searching your local Amazon store for its ASIN - B00QQQ8R2A

Thanks!

All the best

Andy Williams

More Information from Dr. Andy Williams

If you would like more information, tips, tutorials or advice, there are two resources you might like to consider.

The first is my free weekly newsletter over at ezSEONews.com offering tips, tutorials and advice to online marketers and webmasters. Just sign up and my newsletter plus SEO articles will be delivered to your inbox. I cannot always promise a weekly schedule, but I try ;)

I also run a course over at CreatingFatContent.com, where I build real websites in front of members in "real-time" using my system of SEO.

An SEO Checklist

A step-by-step plan for fixing SEO problems with your web site

By Dr. Andy Williams

ezSEONews
Creating Fat Content

Version 1.6
Released: 8th December 2015

What people are saying about this book

"This is the most concise but complete guide to useful SEO that I've seen anywhere since the Google updates." **Karl Steppens**

"Dr. Andy really is an authority on SEO and I highly recommend this book to all webmasters." **DebV**

"This book was very informative and easy to follow. Many great reminders and new information I didn't know." **D Eastman**

"This was a good read because it breaks it down into sections and talks to you like an everyday Joe, so that even inexperienced computer users can see the sense in what is being explained to them." **Miss Winters**

"The author was one of the first "gurus" that I followed, and I've found him well-informed, creative, and generous through the years." **Lane P. Lester**

"Extremely useful information for anyone who has a website or is interested in building one. As always, what I particularly like about Andy's books is that he gives great information which is not padded out with loads of waffle. A good, helpful read." **Linda Plummer**

"What I like is that each issue is explained, so I get to understand why I need to do something. And that legitimate practices are described, so I don't have to worry that Google is going to penalize my website....

... Because it is really a checklist, an actionable one and easy to understand, even you are a non techie like I am." **Francesca CH**

"The author, Andy Williams, is one of the few SEO experts that I listen to as he has integrity, seeks to help people, and offers very useful information." **Jack Raburn**

" I've followed Andy's stuff for many years; he's concise, articulate, precise and careful to give only advice that he's tested himself. This book is in line with all his other guides and information - it's no-fluff, no-BS and thoroughly tested to give you the best advice available right now. If you're lost in the SEO maze, do exactly what he says and you won't believe how easy SEO can be!" **Isobel DeSantis**

DISCLAIMER AND TERMS OF USE AGREEMENT

Why this book?

I've already written an SEO book called **SEO 2015 & Beyond** which is available on Amazon Kindle format, so why this new book?

The original book is an overall strategy for SEO that works. The book is particularly useful for those looking to learn SEO or catch up on recent changes with Google and what that means to the webmaster. However, for many of my students and clients, the biggest problem is where to start on an existing site that has lost its rankings. We've all been there. Everything is going really well, and then you wake up one day to find your Google traffic wiped out. What do you do next?

This book will take you by the hand and guide you through a complete checklist of things you should objectively critique/fix on your website. Now, before I go on, I need to point out that a lot of people are not very objective about their own work. It's often hard to take criticism from other people and even harder to admit that we made a mistake somewhere along the way. However, for this process to work, you need to step outside of yourself and try to view your website as a complete stranger would see it on arrival.

I'd also like to say that although you do need to be critical, I don't want you to be too hard on yourself. Nearly everyone I know lost a site or two in the Google updates of the last 2 years. I lost quite a few myself. The reason why so many people were caught out was the simple fact that Google had moved the goalposts somewhat.

Pre-Panda and pre-Penguin, Google tolerated certain activities. Post-Panda and post-Penguin, they don't. As a result, they are now enforcing their Webmaster Guidelines, something that SEOs never really believed Google would do! It's this change in tolerance that got so many of us into trouble.

Let me give you an example of the moving goal posts.

We have known for some time that Google doesn't like us building backlinks to our site with automated tools. How did we know? Google told us. So why did so many people engage in link-building campaigns using automated tools that created hundreds or thousands of low quality links in a short space of time? The answer is simple. At the time, Google tolerated this behavior and even rewarded it. When you see your competitor building all these links and jumping ahead of you in the search engine results, it's only natural that you want to do the same to get your rankings back, right? I mean Google is rewarding that behavior with better rankings, so it must be OK.

As long as Google openly tolerated this type of link-building, it would continue, and Google knew that.

Google Panda, and probably more specifically Google Penguin, changed all this. Google went from being a very tolerant search engine, to one of zero tolerance and the most recent Penguin update on 22nd May 2013 is the clearest signal of intent from Google.

For as long as I can remember, Google has published Webmaster Guidelines to tell us what they consider acceptable and what is not. Before Panda and Penguin, these were simply that – **guidelines** that we could choose to ignore. With the arrival of Panda and Penguin, these guidelines became **rules**.

All of the "illicit" activities (like link building) that were previously tolerated are now a noose around the neck of the website. Webmasters who may have held the number one spot for years, suddenly found their site gone from page one. Many were even gone from Google altogether.

The reason so many websites lost their rankings was simply because those sites had not followed the guidelines in the past.

I wrote this book to help you more easily identify and fix the problems you may have with your website. It's the same SEO checklist that I use on my student's websites and those of my clients.

How to use this book

I've divided the areas you need to look at into 10 "Checkpoint" chapters. They are:

• Checklist Point #1 – The Domain Name

• Checklist Point #2 – Web Page Real Estate

• Checklist Point #3 – Site Structure

• Checklist Point #4 – Comments

• Checklist Point #5 – Social Presence

• Checklist Point #6 – Would you Trust the site?

• Checklist Point #7 – Bounce Rates & Time on Site

• Checklist Point #8 – Legal pages

• Checklist Point #9 – Content Quality

• Checklist Point #10 – Inbound Link Profiles

These will tell you what you need to be looking out for as well as the theory behind why you need to make these checks. Each Checkpoint chapter ends with a bulleted "checklist" of things you should check in that area.

If you like, you can work your way through the book, checking off each point as you go. However, you might like to read the whole book first and then take action once you understand all of the areas that need your attention.

To make things easier for you, at the end of the book, I've compiled a master checklist that includes all of the checkpoints mentioned throughout the book.

OK, let's start off by looking at what Google actually want.

What does Google want?

Before we start the checklist, I thought it would be a good idea to explain what it is that Google actually wants. You can read their guidelines for yourself, here:

http://support.google.com/webmasters/bin/answer.py?hl=en&answer=35769

Near the top of that page, it says:

> "Even if you choose not to implement any of these suggestions, we strongly encourage you to pay very close attention to the "Quality Guidelines," which outline some of the illicit practices that may lead to a site being removed entirely from the Google index or otherwise impacted by an algorithmic or manual spam action."

It is really important that you take this statement seriously. Google will remove or penalize your site if they catch you carrying out any activities they don't approve of.

To make things worse for anyone trying to fly under the Google radar, they also state:

> "If you believe that another site is abusing Google's quality guidelines, please let us know by filing a spam report."

That phrase "spam report" is hyperlinked to an online form!

Google are trying to get other webmasters to report websites that ignore their guidelines and use shady techniques. That means your competitors can report your site if they see you doing something to cheat the system!

But what do Google consider "illicit practices"?

Here is a list of some things you need to avoid.

• **Pages that are designed for the search engines, not for the visitor**. We've all seen these in the search engine results pages (SERPs). They are pages that are designed with the sole purpose of ranking well in Google, without any care to what the visitor might think when they arrive. Google want engaging, unique content (and I'm talking unique in terms of "voice", discussion or ideas, not just the words and their order on the page).

• **Any trick or "loophole" designed to help a PageRank better in the search engine**. That pretty much covers most of SEO as we used to know it!

• **Content that is auto-created using a software tool**. Most software tools throw out gibberish so this is a fairly obvious point. One type of tool that deserves special attention is article spinners (which gained a lot of followers in the last few years).

Spinners can produce hundreds of near perfect "unique" articles in just a few minutes in the hands of an expert. These spun articles have been used extensively in backlinking campaigns, by many people, but Google are now on the warpath.

Other examples of auto-generated content include articles translated by software (badly) without a human review, scraped content from RSS feeds and "stitching or combining content from different web pages without adding sufficient value." This last point should be of interest to content curators who don't add value to the content they curate.

• **Any "linking schemes" that are designed to manipulate a web PageRank in the search engine.** Wow. That's a big one. Google have told us there that they don't want us building links to our site for the sole purpose of better rankings! But backlinking is one of the most effective ways to improve your rank in Google, so obviously we all do it. Just linking two or more of your own sites together could be considered a linking scheme if the sole point is to help those sites rank better. Other things Google don't like are sites that buy (or sell) links to pass Page Rank (PR), reciprocal linking between sites, and websites that have used automated tools to build backlinks. Google don't even like links inserted into posts you write for other sites (guest posts), if those links are simply there to manipulate your web page rankings.

• **Websites that serve up one version of a page to the search engines, yet a different page to the visitors.** This is called cloaking and is commonly used by webmasters trying to trick the search engines into ranking the "sales" page higher. The page the search engines see is keyword rich (helping the page to rank), whereas the version the visitors see is completely different. Similar to cloaking is "sneaky redirects". This is often achieved with JavaScript or a Meta refresh so that the page the visitor sees is not the same page that the search engine spider crawled and was ultimately ranked for in Google.

• **Pages that have "hidden" text.** In other words, text that is invisible to the visitor. This is commonly done using CSS to make the text the same color as the background. Visitors don't see the text, yet the search engines do (since they read the text based document).

• **Websites that use "doorway pages".** These are poor quality pages that are designed to rank for a single keyword. Sites that employ doorway pages often have hundreds or thousands of them, where their sole purpose is to rank high for a single search term and deliver visitors from the search engine. An example is a website that has lots of pages of similar content, with each page trying to rank for a different geographical location by changing the title and main location based phrases.

• **Affiliate websites that don't add enough value.** These include the typical Amazon affiliate website where each page is a review of a product that links to Amazon. The problem occurs when the review content contains nothing that isn't already found on Amazon or the manufacturers own website. Affiliate sites MUST add significant value.

Some things Google actually recommend you do

• **Use clear, intuitive navigation on your site with text links.** Every page on your site needs to be reachable from a link somewhere on the site. A sitemap helps here (and Google recommends you have one), but it is also a good idea to interlink your content if it helps the visitor navigate your site.

• **Don't have too many links on any given page.** Sites like Wikipedia.org (http://www.wikipedia.org/) seem to ignore this rule yet still rank well for a huge number of searches. However, Wikipedia seems to have been accepted and trusted by Google, so what's good for them may not be good for you.

• **Websites that have useful, information-rich content.** Think here in terms of content written for the visitor, not for the search engine.

• **ALT tags that actually describe the image.** Since ALT tags are often "read" by software for blind visitors, they are very important sources of information for people that cannot actually see the image.

• **Sites should not have broken links.** There is a good free software tool called Xenu Link Sleuth (http://home.snafu.de/tilman/xenulink.html) that can spider your site and check this for you. There really is no excuse.

OK, you get the idea.

We'll look at some of the other things Google like and don't like as we work our way through the checklist, so let's get on with it.

THE SEO CHECKLIST

Checklist Point #1 - The domain name

Exact Match Domains

In the past, keywords in your domain name helped your website rank better. The ultimate ranking boost was from something called an Exact Match Domain or EMD for short. An EMD took keyword "stuffing" to the extreme – by making the domain name the same as the man keyword phrase you are trying to target.

For example, if you wanted to rank well for "buy prescription drugs online", then the exact match domain would be buyprescriptiondrugsonline.XXX where XXX is any one of the domain TLDs (.com, .net, .org etc). Merely having that exact phrase in the domain name gave you an unfair ranking advantage. SEOs soon spotted this and EMDs became hot favorites for anyone trying to make money online.

On 28th September 2012, Matt Cutts (head of Google's webspam team) tweeted the following:

Google had finally decided to take action on "low-quality" EMDs and prevent them from ranking simply because of the phrase in the domain name.

Now, if you have an EMD, don't panic. Google's algorithm changes were designed to remove **low quality EMDs** from the search results, not good sites that happen to be on an EMD (though there is often some collateral damage with big changes to the algorithm, so some good sites were probably hit too). You need to decide if your site is a quality EMD or a low quality one.

Some things to look for that might indicate a low quality EMD site:

• Is the site specifically targeting that EMD phrase or does your site have a lot of quality content within the overall niche?

• Do you have a lot of backlinks with anchor text that matches the EMD phrase?

• Are there very few pages on your site?

• Reading your content, does there appear to be a bias towards using that EMD phrase (to try to help it rank better)?

• Is that EMD phrase repeated a few times on the homepage? What about other pages on the site?

• Is that phrase used in internal links back to the homepage from other pages on the site?

• Is your on-site SEO targeting that EMD phrase?

• Is the EMD phrase one that AdWords Advertisers are willing to bid on? Is it quite commercial?

As an example, here are the estimated costs per click for some contact lens related phrases (as shown in Google's Keyword Tool https://adwords.google.com/o/KeywordTool):

☐	**contact lenses** online order ▾	€5.96
☐	contacts lenses online ▾	€5.65
☐	buy **contact lenses** on line ▾	€5.60
☐	ordering **contact lenses** online ▾	€5.56
☐	order contacts lenses online ▾	€5.55
☐	order contacts online ▾	€5.52
☐	online contacts lenses ▾	€5.52

Any of those phrases turned into an EMD would be suspect.

Take that first phrase as an example. The EMD would be:

contactlensesonlineorder.com

Surely someone would have registered that in the past to take advantage of EMD ranking power? If they could rank for that phrase and slap AdSense ads on the site, then they'd be making a good chunk of change every time someone clicked on an advert.

Typing that domain into my web browser, this is what I get:

Oops! Google Chrome could not find contactlensesonlineorder.com

Suggestions:
- Search on Google:

| contact lenses online order | Google Search |

However, if I search the Way Back Machine (http://web.archive.org), which looks for archived versions of the website, this is what I see:

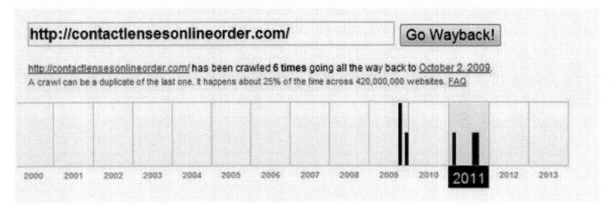

That site existed in 2009, and then again in 2011.

Using Way Back Machine, I can even take a look at that site as it appeared back in 2009 or 2011. Here it is in 2009:

Contact Lenses Online Order

Save up to 70% off retail contact lens prices. Fast, Simple and Cheap.

- Acuvue
- Biomedics
- Freshlook
- Soflens
- Proclear

We carry all popular brands of contact lenses including Acuvue, Biomedics, Focus, Freshlook, Soflens, Purevision, and more. Order your contact lenses, and save up to 70% off contact lens prices.

Best Seller Contact Lenses

Notice the main header on the page uses the exact same phrase. This is typical of low quality EMDs.

So, why is that EMD no longer an active site?

Perhaps Google's plan to wipe out low quality EMDs worked and it no longer made money, so they let it expire? No-one wants it now because of the problems associated with this type of EMD, and the fact that the domain may have picked up a penalty (which isn't always removed when a domain changes hands).

Using Way Back Machine to find problem domains

If your domain has never ranked properly, then I'd recommend that you check it at the Way Back Machine website. You will then be able to see if your domain was used before you got your hands on it. If it was, what was the site like previously? It is possible that a domain could have been penalized in the past, and that domain penalty carried over to the new owner. If this is the case, you could file a reconsideration request at Google (http://support.google.com/webmasters/bin/answer.py?hl=en&answer=35843). While not guaranteed to work, it might if Google can see the domain has changed hands.

Keyword stuffed domains

Another potential problem with a domain name is keyword stuffing.

Let's suppose your website is selling cosmetic contact lenses. If your domain was **cosmetic-halloween-colored-contact-lenses.com** then it's clear that the domain has been stuffed with relevant keywords. This would get you into trouble, but even if it didn't, what would visitors think to a domain like that? This type of domain is not one that I would be anxious to hold on to.

Back in March 2011, Matt Cutts discussed the use of keywords in the domain name in a YouTube video:

http://www.youtube.com/watch?v=rAWFv43qubI

He suggests that a brandable domain is probably better than a keyword rich domain (and I agree). Despite being old, that video hints about the changes to come in the way keyword rich domains are ranked.

Of course, these are just general guidelines on domain names. There isn't much you can do about your domain name once you have it. Your choice is to either stick with it or move your site to a different domain. In this video, Matt Cutts offers some advice on moving a domain:

http://www.youtube.com/watch?v=wATxftE8ooE

The domain name checklist

• EMD? If yes, then be aware that this will work against you and you'll need to de-optimize the site for the phrase in the domain name.

• Keyword stuffed? There isn't much you can do with this other than move the site to a better domain. Keyword stuffed domains look spammy and don't instill much confidence in visitors. Unless there is good reason to keep the domain (like it still makes good income or ranks well), I'd consider moving the site to a better, more brandable domain.

• Has your domain never ranked properly? If not, then check its history at the Way Back Machine. Consider submitting a reconsideration request at Google if it looks like the domain was used by someone else in the past.

Checklist Point #2 – Web page real estate

Above the fold

In January 2012, Google released a document that outlined a new "page layout algorithm improvement". You can read it here:

http://insidesearch.blogspot.com.es/2012/01/page-layout-algorithm-improvement.html

In releasing this change, Google were hoping to improve the user experience. No one likes to arrive at a website if all they see in their browser are Google ads, banners or email subscription forms. The general idea of this update was to penalize sites that didn't have much useful content above the fold. "Above the fold" simply means the viewable area in your browser before you scroll down the page.

In the past, a lot of people made a lot of money throwing up "AdSense sites". These were designed to rank well, but show the visitors very little content, just money-generating adverts. Visitors could either click an advert (and make the webmaster money), click the back button on their browser, or scroll down the page to find the content. Because of the poor user experience on these sites, most people probably opted for one of the first two options as they figured the content would not be up to much. If something caught their eye in the adverts, they'd most probably click there.

NOTE: If you are a member of Google AdSense yourself, you will probably have been told by the AdSense team to put MORE adverts on your pages. The Google AdSense team seems to be at odds with what the Google Search Engine actually wants. Be aware that the two parts work separately and want to achieve different things.

Look at your page above the fold. I'd actually recommend resizing your browser to 1024x768 (most people use this resolution or something higher these days according to W3Schools.com - http://www.w3schools.com/browsers/browsers_display.asp) and seeing what is above the fold on your site.

Once resized, is there meaningful content? If you removed the adverts from that area, would it still offer value to the visitors in terms of the other content above the fold? This is also an interesting test for your page as a whole. If you remove the adverts from a page, would the remaining content be seen as high quality? It should!

NOTE: If you have some adverts above the fold, you may be OK. On the page layout algorithm announcement, Google say:

"This algorithmic change does not affect sites who place ads above-the-fold to a normal degree, but affects sites that go much further to load the top of the

page with ads to an excessive degree or that make it hard to find the actual original content on the page."

Sneaky links in footers, headers or elsewhere

Does your site have links in the footer?

Links *per se* are not a problem, but if they are links with keyword rich anchor text, they could be. If the links in your footer are there simply to make another webpage rank better for a keyword term, then there is a problem.

Look at your footer links. Do they use keyword rich anchor text that the linked to page wants to rank for? If so, remove them.

If you have other footer links to things like Twitter, Facebook, Contact, Privacy etc, then these are fine.

Web page real estate checklist

• Resize your browser to 1024x768 and see what loads above the fold. Is there useful content? Are there too many adverts? If there are too many adverts, especially above the fold, consider removing (or moving) them.

• If you removed all of the adverts from the pages on your site, would those pages still offer the visitor what they are looking for? If not, then the content is not good enough.

• Does your site have sneaky links in the footer, especially keyword rich anchor text links to your own site or an external site? If so, get rid of them.

Checklist Point #3 - Site structure

Is your site navigation helping your visitors find what they want quickly?

If you think in terms of needing every page on your site to be just 1 and a maximum of 2 clicks away from the homepage, then you're on the right track.

Good website navigation should be intuitive to the visitor. They should immediately be able to see where they need to go for the information they require.

A good test here is to ask a friend who has never been to your website to find a particular piece of information. How long does it take them?

Include a search box

I'd highly recommend you have a search box on your website to help people find information. If you are using WordPress, the default search box really is very poor. People won't be able to find what they want on a large site because WordPress doesn't rank its results by any kind of relevance (at least not any that I can detect).

An example

On one of my websites, I had written an article on "vitamin A". I had also referenced vitamin A in 120+ other articles on the site. The WordPress search box placed my main "vitamin A" article around position 125. That's not very good!

WordPress or not, check out the search script your site is using. Do some searches. Does it return the most relevant pages in the results for search queries? If the results are not very good, then you need to look for a new search box script. There is one I can recommend.

What if you could use Google's search engine to power the search box on your site?

Google are kings of search and relevance, so using a search box powered by Google would ensure people find the most relevant pages on your site, quickly and easily. The good news is you can. After installing it on the site I mentioned above, and searching for "vitamin A", my main article came up #1, just as it should do.

You can find out more about Google Custom Search here:

http://www.google.com/cse/

If you have an AdSense account, you can create the search box within that account to use on your site. It will have AdSense ads in the search results, but you do make money when the adverts are clicked. If you want to opt-out of the adverts in your custom search engine, visit the link above because Google do have a paid option for this.

Site-wide links

Site-wide links are links that appear on all pages of your site. You do actually have to be careful and not overdo them. If you do have site-wide links, they should not use keyword phrases you are trying to rank for.

NOTE: Site-wide links can be to pages on your own website or a different website.

In the past, swapping site-wide links with webmasters of other sites has been a common SEO practice, but I am saying don't do it. Google's quality guidelines clearly state that IF these are an attempt to manipulate search rankings, then they should be avoided.

If you are a WordPress site owner, typical site-wide links that comes pre-installed with WordPress include the blogroll. I recommend you remove this from your site, even if you have edited it with more relevant websites.

Site-wide links are typically found in the header, footer or sidebar of the site. One of the most common forms of site-wide links is the main menu of the site. This menu links to the main areas of the website and serves a useful purpose. I would recommend that your main navigation menu is not keyword-focused, and instead, is written with the visitor in mind to help them find what they are looking for.

On smaller sites (10 or so pages), the main navigation menu usually links to all of the pages on the site. Again, avoid keyword-rich anchor text in these menus and always think what is most helpful to the visitor.

As your site grows, it becomes unnatural to link to all pages on your site from the main menu found on every page. A far better strategy is to create individual menus for each section of your site, and put these menus on the pages in those sections. Let's consider "context-sensitive navigation".

Context-sensitive navigation

The navigation system on your site can include menus in:

• The header

• The footer

• The sidebar

• Within the content area, usually at the end of a particular piece of content.

On larger websites, the navigation system you use should not be the same on every page of the site. The navigation should change depending on the page being visited. I'm not suggesting every page on your site has a different navigation menu, but certainly sections of your site could use their own custom menu.

The easiest way to think about this is with an example. If you had a h'
the visitor is on a page about osteoporosis, a menu that could help t'
contain links to other articles about osteoporosis. You could still inclu.
"block" linking to the main areas within the site, but you'd also include mo..
options for your visitor, related to the current article they are reading.

Let's consider another example. If you had a travel site and a visitor was on a page talking about restaurants in Bali, it would make sense to have navigation options that show other articles on Bali, maybe hotels, attractions, surfing, etc.

What if you have an ecommerce site selling baby products? You might have a main site-wide menu that includes links to all of the main sections on your site – strollers, cots, car seats, etc, but when your visitor is browsing the section on strollers, a menu with links to 2-seat strollers, jogging strollers, etc would be very helpful. Always think in terms of how your navigation can best serve your visitors.

This type of dynamic navigation is clearly easier and more practical to implement on larger sites. However, if you have a small site with a site-wide menu, do look at your navigation and make sure your links are not keyword-focused and that the navigation HELPS the visitor.

A tip for WordPress users

Two plugins I recommend for helping you create a dynamic navigation system are:

• **Dynamic widgets.** (http://wordpress.org/extend/plugins/dynamic-widgets/). This allows you to setup different sidebar menus (created as widgets) in different areas of your site.

• **Yet Another Related Posts Plugin (YARPP).**

http://wordpress.org/extend/plugins/yet-another-related-posts-plugin/

This allows you to setup a related posts section after each piece of content. When a visitor gets to the end of an article, they'll see a list of related articles and be tempted to click through to one. This type of internal linking is also beneficial from a search engine perspective as it links related content together.

Content organization on your server (non-WordPress sites)

Organization of your content on the server and your site's navigation system go hand-in-hand. One mirrors the other. Well organized content is stored in a logical, intuitive manner, which is reflected in the navigation system.

The physical organization on your server is only important if you are building your website using something like HTML, which stores as webpage as a discrete file. It therefore doesn't apply to WordPress (WordPress does not save content as individual files).

Let's use a theoretical example of a pet website. It might have content written about:

- Fish

- Birds

- Dogs

- Reptiles

- Amphibians

- Cats

There should be a folder/directory on your server for each of these content areas, and all content should be saved into the corresponding folder. Can you see how this physical organization would mirror the navigation system of the site?

The first thing for you to check is whether or not your content is properly organized into folders on your server. Are all dog related articles physically located within a dog folder (aka a directory) on your server?

As the dog section on the site grows, we'll need to add to the structure of the folders/directories on our server to re-organize our content, in the exact same way that we did with the navigation system earlier.

For example, if your site was an informational site, you could add the following sub-folders under your "dog" folder on the server:

- Training

- Toys

- Beds

- Food & treats

Each of these would then store the content related to those folders. So for example, all articles on dog training would be located in the "/dogs/training/" folder on your server.

If your site sold pets, perhaps a more logical way to organize the content would be to have sub-folders like:

- Alsatians

- Terriers

- Dalmatians

• Huskies

.. And so on.

By organizing your content into logical folders on your server, the URLs of these pages would be like this:

mypetsite.com/dogs/training/clickers.html

mypetsite.com/dogs/training/choke-chain.html

mypetsite.com/dogs/training/walking-to-heel.html

mypetsite.com/dogs/food/mixers.html

mypetsite.com/dogs/food/tinned-dog-food.html

mypetsite.com/dogs/food/snacks.html

These URLs give the search engines big clues about the content. For example, the search engines would know that all 6 of those web pages were about dogs. It would also know that three were related to training dogs, while three were related to dog food.

This type of physical organization helps the search engines categorize and rank your content because your pages end up in "silos" of related content (with links between related content).

This folder organization on your server should match the menu navigation on your site.

NOTE: If you are using WordPress, you can get the same types of URLs by using categories. While categories are not physical locations like directories/folders on the server, the do serve the same purpose in categorizing your content into logical groups.

WordPress actually takes things a stage further and includes a feature called tags. You can think of tags as an additional way to classify your content, the main way being with categories. I won't go into how to use WordPress categories and tags in this book, other than to give you two quick tips:

1. Never use a word or phrase as both a category and a tag. If it's a really important part of your site structure it's a category. If it's less important, use a tag.
2. Never use a tag if it will only ever be used on one post. If a tag is important, it will be used on several posts on your site. If it's not, it's not important, therefore delete it.

Internal linking of content

When one of your pieces of content references information that is found somewhere else on your site, it makes sense to link to that other page within the body of your content. If we look at this Wikipedia page you can see a lot of links:

Although oxidation reactions are crucial for life, they can also be damaging; plants and animals maintain complex systems of multiple types of antioxidants, such as glutathione, vitamin C, vitamin A, and vitamin E as well as enzymes such as catalase, superoxide dismutase and various peroxidases. Insufficient levels of antioxidants, or inhibition of the antioxidant enzymes, cause oxidative stress and may damage or kill cells.

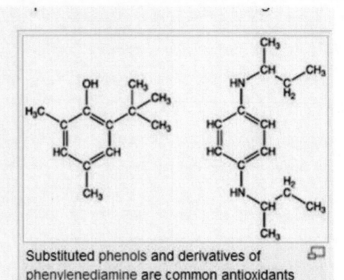

Substituted phenols and derivatives of phenylenediamine are common antioxidants used to inhibit gum formation in gasoline (petrol).

Each of these links goes to another web page on the Wikipedia website. I've circled one hyperlink where the anchor text is "glutathione". This link jumps to the page on Wikipedia all about "glutathione". Not only does this help the search engine spider to index the pages on your site, it also helps the visitor to navigate more easily. Anyone reading this article that doesn't know what glutathione is could click the link and read about it before returning to the original page to continue reading.

Internal linking helps visitors, and it also help the search engines. Links with anchor text tell the search engine what the page is about. The only recommendation I'd make with internal linking is that you vary the anchor text in those links, much like you do with external links pointing into your website.

I did an experiment on internal linking and published my results here on my site:

http://ezseonews.com/backlinks/internal-linking-seo/

The article gives you tips on using internal linking, plus results of an experiment I ran.

Essentially I took one of my websites that ranked at #190 for a particular phrase I was targeting. Using nothing but internal links, I managed to move that page up to #14 in

Google. That to me indicates that Google like internal linking when it's done to help the visitor (and it clearly helps your pages rank better).

The things I'd recommend you look at on your own site are:

1. Do you make use of internal linking in the body of the content like Wikipedia?
2. Do you vary internal link anchor texts to a specific page?
3. For any particular anchor text, make sure you only ever link to one URL using it. Using the same anchor text to point to two or more different URLs is confusing, especially for the search engines.

Site structure checklist

• Is your navigation intuitive?

• Are all of the pages on your site just one or two clicks away from the homepage?

• Do you have site-wide links in the sidebar?

• Do you have site-wide links in the header?

• Do you have site-wide links in the footer?

NOTE: Site-wide links with keyword-rich anchor text are the most potentially damaging.

• If you have a large site, do you use dynamic menus, which change depending on the section of the site the visitor is viewing?

• Do you have a search box? If it is a WordPress default search box, I highly recommend you switch to a more efficient script, e.g. Google's custom search.

• Do you internally link the pages of your website from within the body of your content, not just via the navigation menus or a related posts menu?

• Is your content organized logically into "silos" where all related content is in the same category or folder? If necessary (e.g. on a large site), do you use sub-folders to help make the navigation even more intuitive?

• If you are using WordPress, do you have tags that are only used once or twice? If so, remove them.

• If you are using WordPress, do you have tags that are identical to some of your categories? Never use a phrase for a tag if it is being used (or will be used) as a category.

Checklist Point #4 – Comments

Visitor contact

A visitor-friendly site is one that offers your visitors the chance to interact with you.

Something ALL websites should have is a contact form.

Something else that I highly recommend you include is a comment form where visitors can comment on your content. Obviously, this may not be applicable in all cases, but visitors do like to know there is a real person behind a site and often like to give their opinions as well. Not only does a comment form build trust, it also builds social proof as new visitors can see that other people have left comments on your site.

There are contact form scripts and comment form scripts available for HTML websites. Content management systems like WordPress have the comments built in, and contact forms are readily available as plugins.

I recommend you implement both on your site if it makes sense to do so.

If you already have a comment form on your site, check the comment settings. If you have your comments set to auto-approve, then set it to "administrator approval" so that ALL comments need to go by you first. If you set up comments for auto-approval, you'll get a lot of spam comments that bring the quality of your site down, and could themselves cause a penalty if these comments link to "bad neighborhoods".

Bad neighborhoods?

Let me explain.

Most spammers leave comments with the sole intention of getting a backlink to their own web site. Many of these will be low quality sites, porn sites, or other types of sites that you would not want to associate with your own. These types of sites are referred to as "bad neighborhoods" by Google. In addition, there is nothing to stop someone who has left a comment on your site (and had it approved some time ago), from redirecting their link to a bad neighborhood at a later date. To be safe, make comments on your site **nofollow**.

Once everything is set up properly, go through **every single comment** on your site and delete any that are either fake or spam.

Fake comments

Fake comments are those that you or someone you asked (or hired) wrote. A lot of webmasters add fake comments to their own site to make the site look a little more active. Don't do it. Fake comments are often easily spotted and don't instill trust once you've been rumbled.

Typical ways that fake comments stand out are:

1. Several comments posted within a very short time of one another and then nothing, at least for a while.
2. Groups of fake comments rarely have author images associated with the comment (Gravatars) which makes them stand out even more.
3. Comments are "bland" and don't really add anything to the content.
4. Comments are copied from another website, e.g. Amazon.

Spam comments

Spam comments are not always easy to spot. They are left with the sole intention of getting a valuable backlink, so spammers have become creative in the way they do their spamming. There are even software tools to help them carry out mass-scale spamming of comment-enabled websites.

As a general rule, don't approve any comment that is "stroking your ego", or "patting you on the back for a job well done".

One way spammers try to get their comments approved is to say things like "Great article" or "This is amazing, I've told my friends about this". Here is one I got the other day:

> Submitted on 2013/03/05 at 08:42
>
> You blog post is just completely quality and informative. Many new facts and information which I have not heard about before. Keep sharing more blog posts.

While I have no doubt that this comment is true ;) sadly it is spam.

This flattery is supposed to stroke the ego of the webmaster so it gets through the approval process. Don't approve it, UNLESS you know the comment is legitimate i.e. you recognize the commenter.

Comment spam can also be cleverly disguised.

For example, a spammer might find a page they want a backlink from on the "health benefits of zinc". They'll then go and find an article on the web about this topic and grab a quote from that article to use as a comment. The quote will look like a real comment about your article, but will in fact be content copied from another website. This type is often difficult to catch, except to say that most cases don't quite look right in the context of your article. If in doubt, grab the content of the comments, put it in quotes, and search Google for it.

Another type of comment spam is where the commenter is just trying to get traffic to their own website. Here is an example of that:

Submitted on 2013/03/08 at 13:34

I would certainly not recommend 1&1. My recent experiences are detailed on my blog, here;

I have always found Bluehost easy to use, Hostgator I find a little "clunky" but my favourite has to be Dreamhost. They had a few issues in the past but everything works like a dream for me and I find their unique control panel interface so easy to use.

You can see I've blurred out the URL linking to his web page.

His page is basically a review of his favorite web hosting company (which does include his experiences with 1&1), and an affiliate link to that host. He left a comment that I would have otherwise approved, but not with that link to his web page. He is probably targeting any "high traffic" website that has reviewed the 1&1 web host, or even Hostgator, and leaving similar reviews in the hope he can piggy-back their traffic as well as benefit from the relevant backlink.

General rule for approving comments

Only approve comments if:

1. It is clear from the comment that the person has read the article.
2. The comment adds something to the article, like another point of view.
3. If you know that the person is real because you recognize their name (but only if the comment is also not spammy).

Obviously these are just guidelines. In the field of battle, you'll have to make some tough decisions, but I recommend only keeping the best comments that you're sure are genuine. Delete EVERYTHING else.

Comments checklist

• Does your website have a comments section where visitors can leave comments, thoughts and questions?

• Does your website have a contact us form?

• If you have comments enabled, are you manually approving all comments? You should be.

• Check through all of the comments on your site and remove any fake or spam comments. In fact, remove any comment whose sole purpose is to get a backlink to a website.

• Make comment links nofollow.

• Going forward, only approve legitimate comments where it is clear the visitor has read your content and added to the conversation with their insight.

Checklist Point #5 – Social presence

Under the umbrella of social presence, I include two things:

• The website/website author has a social presence on social media sites.

• The website has social sharing "buttons" on the site to allow visitors to share the content to their social media followers.

Check your website. Do you have both of these?

Let's look to see exactly what I mean, as well as give you some ideas for a "bare minimum" social approach.

The website/website author has a social presence

The three main social channels I'd recommend you look at are:

1. Facebook
2. Twitter
3. Google Plus

I would probably recommend you consider these in that order as well. If you have a Facebook account you can easily setup a Facebook Page for your website. You can then link to the Facebook page from your site.

You can see how I have this setup on one of my sites. Visitors can follow me on Twitter, Facebook or add me to a circle on Google plus.

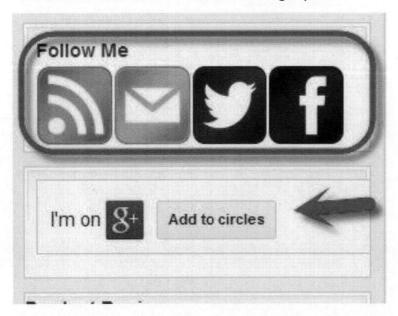

Your Facebook page offers your visitors an additional channel for starting a "conversation" with you. From your point of view, you can post updates to that page which include things like:

- Tips and tricks for your industry/niche.

- Current news in your niche.

- Interesting articles you find around the web.

- New posts on your site (this can be automated).

- Videos, images etc.

- Current special offers from your website.

- Anything else that is relevant to your site and niche.

Think of your Facebook page as an extension of your website. A Facebook page that has a thriving community can rank well in Google, plus give your "brand" a huge amount of social proof. It's so easy to setup, I recommend all websites have a Facebook page.

As far as Twitter is concerned, it's also very easy to setup an account for your website. You can even setup your website to automatically send a tweet to your Twitter account, every time new content is published on your site. You can of course also send tweets with information related to your niche (the same kind of stuff that you can post on Facebook). Services like Hootsuite (http://hootsuite.com) allow you to schedule tweets (as well as Facebook and Google Plus posts) in advance.

As your Twitter following increases, you'll automatically be increasing your "authority" in the eyes of your visitors. Let's face it, if you have a Twitter account with 10,000+ followers, a lot of people will think "Wow, this site must be good".

Now, before you tell me that you've tried Twitter and only ever managed to get a handful of followers, there are ways to increase the number of followers. I wrote an article called "How to get more Twitter Followers" (http://ezseonews.com/review/how-to-get-more-twitter-followers/) and I have used the methods described there to consistently build Twitter lists into the thousands. While it's true that your Twitter list may not be too responsive when built that way, that's not really the point. The main point of this to begin with is social proof on your site. As your site grows in authority, your Twitter following will increase naturally with more targeted individuals. It then becomes more than just a social proof thing. It becomes a useful tool for business.

When you have a Twitter account, make sure you link to it from your website so that people can follow you on Twitter (as I did in the previous screenshot). Once your Twitter following has grown to the point where you are proud of it, you may want to head on over to http://twittercounter.com and get a "badge" for your site. The badge displays how many Twitter followers you've got. This all helps add authority to your site, and the more authority your site is given by visitors, the more authority it is given by the search engines which monitor visitor behavior.

The final social media platform that I recommend getting involved with is Google Plus. You can setup a Google Plus "Page" for your website and post to it, in much the same way you do to Facebook. Google plus works in a very different way though, and it's beyond the scope of this book to teach you Google Plus.

OK, those are the social media channels that I suggest you get involved in.

Let's see how you can give your visitors the opportunity to share your content with their followers – using social sharing buttons.

The website has social sharing "buttons"

If I show you an example, I am sure you'll recognize what I am talking about:

Typically, social media sharing buttons appear in a "panel", either above, below (or above AND below) the content on the page. This panel can be horizontal or even floating vertically (as in the screenshot above), over the webpage on the right or left, or in a sidebar.

In my screenshot, the top one is Facebook, the second Twitter and the third Google Plus. Again, I'd recommend concentrating on these three.

NOTE: The bottom one in the screenshot is another service called Buffer, which isn't currently on my essential list. It could be in the future though, so you may want to read up on that service here:

http://bufferapp.com/

Other social media sites you might like to have buttons for include Pinterest (if your site has a lot of images that you want shared) and StumbleUpon.

For WordPress users, there are a stack of plugins to add this functionality to a site.

For HTML sites, you'll need to find a script that has these features, or manually go to each social media site and grab the button code to include in your own social media "panel".

What do these buttons do exactly?

These buttons give visitors to your site the opportunity to share your webpage with their social media followers.

For example, if I clicked on the Tweet button in the panel above, a Tweet would be constructed automatically with the URL and title of that page.

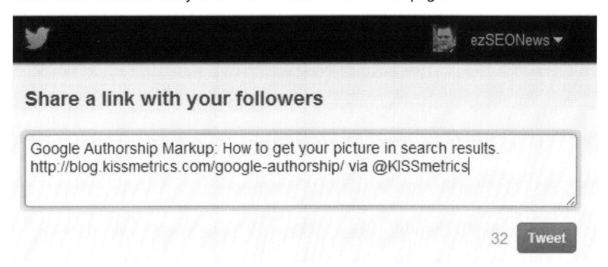

You'll see at the end of the Tweet that Twitter has added "via @KISSmetrics". This sends "KISSmetrics" (the author of the content) a notification that I have tweeted their content. This is one way you can connect with the leaders in your niche.

When you have these social share buttons on your site, your visitors become your army of promoters, as long as your content is good.

So, check your site. Do you have social sharing buttons? If not, I highly recommend you add them (at least for the main three).

NOTE: Google do index tweets and probably use them as a social signal in ranking (although probably only for a limited time). Google also knows how many Facebook likes your content gets and may use that as a social signal. And of course, Google obviously monitor Google pluses.

Social presence checklist

• Does the website have a presence on Facebook?

• Does the website have a presence on Twitter?

• Does the website have a presence on Google plus?

• Does your website have social sharing buttons that allow your visitors to share your content with their social media followers? You should include Twitter, Facebook and Google plus as a bare minimum.

• Setup Google Authorship for your site, connecting your content to your Google plus profile.

Checklist Point #6 – Would you trust the site?

This section looks at the trust levels for your site. We've already discussed some of the things that can help people trust your site, but let's look at a more comprehensive list.

People like to deal with real people. So when they arrive at your site, do they know who they are dealing with?

A photo

A lot of split testing has shown that a photo of a real person increases conversions. From my own experience, the photos that work the best are NOT the ones that look like "stock photos", but those that look like a real person, the person next door. There's a reason for that. Websites that show real people help to build trust. When someone trusts your site, they are more likely to follow through with your call to action.

So where are the best places to put a photo on your site? Well it really depends on the type of site you have, but a photo in the header or the sidebar can work. Here is one found in a sidebar:

Do you see how Shane looks like a real person in that photo?

The style of Shane's photo is very different from many of the photo's you'd get from a stock photo site:

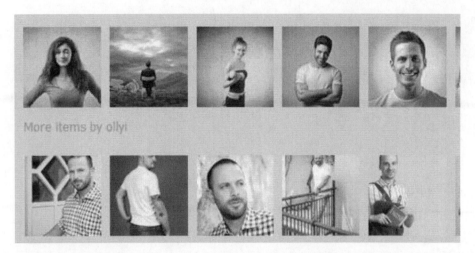

Whichever photo you use, make sure you look like a real person and not a photographic model. People want to trust the photo and anything that looks too glitzy could be seen as fake.

My favorite place to include a photo is in an author's resource box at the end of each piece of content. Here is an example:

There's a separate case in progress that may lead to the Microsoft patent being ruled invalid, but that doesn't appear to have any bearing on this case at the moment.

A final decision is expected in May.

Related Entries
- Google In Privacy Flap With Germans Over New iOS Maps
- Google, Microsoft Cooperate To Invalidate Broad Online Mapping Patent

Related Topics: Google: Legal | Google: Maps & Local | Google: Outside US | Legal: Patents | Top News

About The Author: Matt McGee is Editor-In-Chief of Search Engine Land. His news career includes time spent in TV, radio, and print journalism. His web career continues to include a small number of SEO and social media consulting clients, as well as regular speaking engagements at marketing events around the U.S. He blogs at Small Business Search Marketing and can be found on Twitter at @MattMcGee and/or on Google Plus. You can read Matt's disclosures on his personal blog. See more articles by Matt McGee

Connect with the author via: Email | Twitter | Google+ | LinkedIn

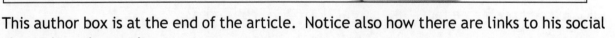

This author box is at the end of the article. Notice also how there are links to his social channels underneath.

If you don't have a photograph of the author or owner on your site, I'd recommend you add one ASAP.

About Us page

Every website should have an About Us page and those that do, often find it's one of the most visited pages on the site. The About Us page is something that many of us skip over and ignore, but it really does help to build trust when people can find out more about you and your site. It also gives you an opportunity to let your visitors understand you on a more human level. What drives you and the site? That can be very important on dry, technical types of sites. If you want more advice on how to create an "About Us" page, I recommend you read this article:

http://socialmediatoday.com/bryan-eisenberg/1006526/about-us-page-social-world

Bryan Eisenberg offers some great advice and even gets you started by answering some simple questions.

Comments enabled

We've already talked about comments earlier in this book. Make sure you have a comment system installed on your site so that visitors can leave feedback. Good feedback can only help build trust and social proof for you and your brand.

Does the site pretend to be a merchant?

This specifically refers to affiliate sites who send traffic to a merchant site in return for making commissions on any sale.

Some affiliate marketers don't make it clear that they are an intermediary in the sales process, rather than the actual merchant.

E.g. the marketers may use links that say "Buy here" or "Buy now" without letting customers know they'll be visiting a different site to complete the transaction. Look at it from a visitor point of view. Don't you think it's a bit of a shock to be on one site, click the "buy" button, and then end up on say Amazon, for example? Sure it is.

Is the site/webmaster a recognized authority?

Being an authority basically means you are recognized as someone to trust in your niche. It's something you can achieve relatively easily if you do one thing:

BE EVERYWHERE!

Part of the reason I look for a social presence from the websites I critique is because these help to build your authority. If someone finds your Facebook page (where they see your photo) in Google, and likes it, then when they go to your website (and see your photo) they think, "hmmm, I've seen this person before and they know what they're talking about." The same goes for any social media channel (as long as you only share quality information to those channels).

One method I use to extend my reach into a niche is to use the same photograph (either me, or the persona for that site), on my site, my Facebook, Twitter & Google+ pages, PLUS, and this is a big one, as a Gravatar (http://en.gravatar.com/), which is set up on the main email address for the site. A Gravatar is just an image associated with an email address. Whenever you post on forums, or comment on Gravatar-enabled blogs, your photo is shown next to your post. People will start to recognize you everywhere they go within that niche, because you are "Everywhere". If the information your share through these channels is good, you can quickly build a reputation as someone to trust, an authority figure in your niche.

NOTE: Being a recognized authority is particularly important on medical sites. You need to know what you are talking about first and foremost, but secondly, people need to trust you. If you are a doctor, or have specific training related to your site, let your visitors know.

If your site is related to health or medicine, are you a recognized authority? If not, then that is something you might like to work on.

Other reasons people don't trust your website?

There are a few other reasons why people won't trust a website. I won't go into details on each of these reasons, I'll just list them. If they are missing from your own website, then maybe you'll consider adding them.

• No Contact page.

• No privacy page.

• No business address or phone number clearly displayed.

• Doesn't seem to have been updated in years.

• No testimonials.

• Copyright notice on the website is out of date.

• Lack of "trust symbols", e.g. Better Business Bureau, VeriSign, McAfee, etc.

• Web pages with typos, spelling mistakes or grammatical errors.

• Lack of response from YOU where comments/questions have been posted.

• Bad reviews.

• Poorly targeted emails, and difficulty unsubscribing from your newsletter.

Trust checklist

• Does the site have a photo of the webmaster/author of the content?

• Does your site have an About Us page?

• Are Comments enabled?

• Does your site pretend to be a merchant?

• Is the author of your site a recognized authority in the niche/industry?

• Are you using a Gravatar setup on the email address you use for your site?

• Is your business address displayed on the site, preferably with a phone number?

• When was the last time your site was updated?

• If appropriate, are there testimonials and are they up to date?

• Does the copyright notice on your website display the correct year?

• Do you display any trust symbols (if appropriate)

• Check all content for spellings and grammatical errors. Check your navigation systems for these errors as well.

• Are there unanswered comments on your site?

Checklist Point #7 - Bounce rates & time on site

There are two metrics that Google most certainly monitor as a way of determining visitor satisfaction levels. The first is the bounce rate and the second is the time they spend on your site.

According to Google:

> *"Bounce rate is the percentage of visits that go only one page before exiting a site."*

In other words, someone only views one page on your site before exiting. Typically, high bounce rates are seen as bad. It may mean that people are not finding what they want on your site.

Time on site is the length of time a visitor stays on your site. A low time on site may indicate a problem with your content, since people aren't sticking around to read it.

The problem is, Google Analytics does not accurately report bounce rates or time on site. Rather than explain, you can read this article on the topic which also contains a fix:

http://briancray.com/posts/time-on-site-bounce-rate-get-the-real-numbers-in-google-analytics/

I recommend you implement the change suggested in that article. You'll then have a better idea of your true bounce rates and visitor time on site.

Once the change is set up, leave your site to collect new data for a month or so before trying to analyze these metrics. Then, go through your analytics to find pages that have high bounce rates AND low time spent on the page(s).

A page with a high bounce rate but high time on the page is not a problem. Look at these examples:

Avg. Time on Page	Entrances	Bounce Rate ↓
00:52:18	3	66.67%
00:00:00	2	50.00%
00:17:41	2	50.00%
00:00:00	4	50.00%

The top page in the list has a bounce rate of 66.67% (the site average is around 10% so 66.67% is high). Despite the high bounce rate, I am happy with this page because there were three visitors, with an average time on that page of 52 minutes 18 seconds. This tells me that the visitor must have found the information useful and engaging.

Similarly, the second page I highlighted above has a bounce rate of 50% with two visits. However, the average time on that page was 17 minutes 41 seconds, so again, those two visitors must have found what they wanted (or at least found it interesting) before they hit their back button to go back to Google.

The two pages that would worry me are the examples that I haven't circled. Both pages had an average time on site of 0 minutes. I would go and look at these pages in more depth, and over a longer period of time, to see whether there may have been a glitch in the reporting during the above screenshot, or whether these pages historically have high bounce rates and a low time on the page.

What you need to so is identify pages with high bounce rate AND low time on the page and see if you can work out why visitors are not satisfied with what they see. If the content is good, maybe it's just not a good match for the search phrase they used to find you in Google. Maybe something else is pushing them away from your site? You need to look for ways to increase the visitor time on these pages (and hopefully decrease bounce rate).

Bounce rate & time on site checklist

I recommend you install the updated code here (which will give you a more accurate measurement of these parameters):

http://briancray.com/posts/time-on-site-bounce-rate-get-the-real-numbers-in-google-analytics/

Once installed and allowed to run for a few weeks, check your bounce rate and time on site at Google Analytics.

• Are your average bounce rates high?

• Are visitors spending a long or short time on your site?

• Look for specific pages where bounce rate is high AND time on site is low. Try to work out why these pages are suffering and fix them accordingly.

Checklist Point #8 – Legal pages

There are certain pages on a website that I call "legal" pages. These are things like:

• Privacy

• Disclaimers (including any medical or earnings disclaimers).

• Contact Us

• Terms

• About Us (we talked about this earlier in terms of visitor trust).

• Any other documents that should be displayed on your site. These might include things like cookie policy, anti-spam policy, outbound link disclaimer and so on.

Does your website include all of the necessary documents?

This article will help you decide which legal documents you need:

http://www.seqlegal.com/blog/what-legal-documents-do-i-need-my-new-website

They also offer webmasters free "legal" documents here:

http://www.seqlegal.com/free-legal-documents

There are "credits" written into these documents that need to be left in place, but for a small fee (currently £3.50), you can get that credit removed.

Legal pages checklist

Not all of these pages are necessary for all types of website, so check which pages your site needs and add them if they are missing.

• Do you have a privacy page?

• Do you have a disclaimer page?

• Do you have a terms of use and conditions page (TOS)?

• Do you have a contact page?

• Do you have an about us page?

• Do you have a medical disclaimer page?

• Do you have an email policy page?

• Do you have an outbound link policy page?

Checklist Point #9 - Content quality

This is a huge component of modern SEO.

If your content is bad, then getting everything else right won't fix the site.

You need to have a website that you are proud of. More than that, you need to have a website that you would be proud to show anyone at Google. Content is what separates an average site from a great site and the best way to understand what Google is looking for is to ask yourself:

"Could the content appear in a magazine?"

This question was actually taken from the Google blog when discussing quality content, so it's what you should be aiming for.

Obviously ecommerce sites have a lot of pages that wouldn't satisfy this question, but it's a great question to ask on any article-based content.

Here is another question that can apply to most types of content:

"Is your content the type of content that people will want to bookmark, or share socially?"

NOTE: Google can certainly detect bookmarks and social shares, so they are able to use them as indicators if they choose to.

The biggest problem I have found concerning content quality is that webmasters are not very impartial when judging their own. If you can, it's always better to get someone else to evaluate your content.

Besides the quality of your content, there are a number of things to look out for as you assess the content on your website. Here is a checklist (in no particular order):

• Has the content been copied and published by other websites?

This is a common problem, though setting up Google Authorship for your site should keep your content safer moving forward. To check whether your content has been stolen, you could use a site like Copyscape (http://www.copyscape.com). Alternatively, grab a sentence or two from your web page and search for it on Google between quotes. Google will then tell you whether that text is found on any other website(s). Here is an example of what it looks like when you do this type of search and other sites have copied your content:

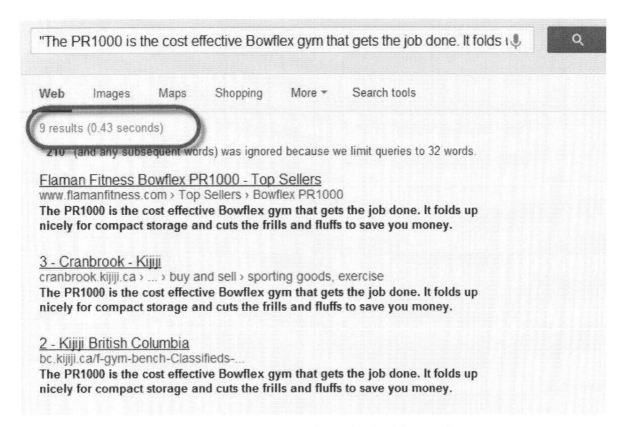

See how there are 9 results in Google, each with the identical text.

If other sites have stolen your content and used it on their own sites, I'd recommend setting up Google authorship immediately, if you haven't already. Next, contact those other sites and ask them to take the content down as it's breaching your copyright. Usually the threat of getting their hosting company involved is enough for most people to remove your stuff. Here is an article written by Jim Edwards that addresses the problem of copyright infringement:

http://ezseonews.com/general/internet-copyright-infringement-and-how-to-handle-it/

The article is a little old, but it still has great advice.

If you prefer, you can hire services to deal with content thieves. http://www.dmca.com is one; although I've never used them, so cannot personally vouch for their service.

- **Product reviews unbiased?**

If you have product reviews on your site, are they unbiased, or positive, positive and more hyped up positives? You need to share both sides of the story and ALL products have some things that are not perfect.

- **More than just a rehash of the merchant site content?**

On the topic of reviews, is the content just a rehash of what you can find on the merchant site or perhaps Amazon? Your reviews need to be PERSONAL. Readers must know that you have personally tried the product and therefore your review must contain insights not seen on ANY other website. Write your review from personal experience.

- **Affiliate link disclaimer?**

If your site is an affiliate site, do you have an affiliate link disclaimer? Do people on your site know you are not the merchant?

This all comes back to the issue of trust. I realize that an affiliate link disclaimer can hurt conversion rates, so try to find a way to tell your visitors in such a way that they don't mind you being an affiliate. After all, you are helping them with their buying decision, aren't you?

In my experience, if someone reads an impartial review that was obviously written by someone that had used the product, they don't mind clicking a link knowing it's an affiliate link. If they read a hyped up sales pitch and then find out your link is an affiliate link, then good luck with that.

- **Keyword stuffing**

Keyword stuffing is a really bad SEO crime. In the past, webmaster knew that adding keywords to their content would make it rank better for those keywords, and articles often became stuffed with keyword phrases. Today, that kind of thing will get your site penalized or even booted out of Google altogether.

As you read your content, ask yourself if it was written for a human or a search engine. If the latter, then re-write it or scrap it altogether.

A quick test for stuffing is to read your content carefully (or get a friend to read it). Can you pick out phrases you think the article was designed to rank for because of the way it repeats a phrase, or slight grammatical errors that were left in just so a particular phrase could be inserted?

All keyword stuffed content MUST be removed. Whether that means re-writing it or deleting it, that's your choice.

My advice when you are writing content is WRITE NATURALLY!

If you hear anyone talking about keyword densities, ignore them. The correct density for any word or phrase on a page is the density that it ends up as when written naturally. It might be 2%, it might be 1%, and it might even be 0.1% or 0%. Bear that in mind. As you read your content, try to see if any word or phrase seems to be used more than is natural.

- **Fluff rating**

Fluff rating is a term I use with my students.

Looking at the http://www.thefreedictionary.com/fluff, fluff is defined as:

Something of little substance or consequence, *especially:*

a. Light or superficial entertainment: The movie was just another bit of fluff from Hollywood.

b. Inflated or padded material: The report was mostly fluff, with little new information.

Part (b) is exactly what I am referring to - an article that goes on and on but doesn't really say anything.

Webmasters have typically tried to increase the length of their content because they think that longer content ranks better. This means that an article that could be covered in just 400 words in a quality piece is stretched out to 600 words - 200 of which are fluff, and only there to raise the word count.

Fluffy content is often found on websites that outsource their content creation. The webmaster asks the writer for a certain word count (since articles are bought on a per word basis), so may request a 600 word article, irrespective of whether the topic NEEDS 600 words or not. The writer then struggles to find 600 words worth of content, so pads it out with fluff.

An article that says very little despite the word count, has a high fluff rating and should be deleted or re-written to provide quality information on a given topic.

- **Information duplicated on multiple articles**

Does information on one page of your site appear on other pages as well? In other words, is there overlap between the content on the various pages of your site? If so, you need to remove it. If two or more articles are closely related enough to share the same information, consider merging those pieces into one big article.

The pages on a website should all contain different information and there should be a bare minimum of content overlap.

- **Check the sitemap**

A sitemap is a great way to check your content. As you look through the sitemap, are there instances where two pages have very similar filenames, or titles? If so, are those two pages covering the same information? If yes, consider combining them into a single quality article?

A common strategy for building a website is to carry out keyword research and then write content around the keywords that have high demand and low competition. One problem with this approach is that two or more phrases - that basically mean the same thing - often become the basis for separate articles.

A site might have separate articles based on each of these phrases:

• Best vacuum

• Best vacuum cleaner

• Which is the best vacuum?

Can you see how those three phrases are saying the same thing? So how can there be three separate articles for these phrases?

Here is an example I found on one website:

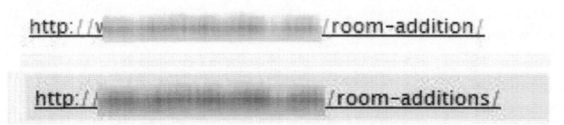

This website has an article on "room addition" and another on "room additions". Really?

Here is another example:

The mood of the party is set right at the beginning.

Baby Shower Invitation Idea
Here is a fun baby shower invitation idea to help cr
occasion.

Baby Shower Invitation
A great baby shower invitation for the internet age.

Baby Shower Invite
Since the baby shower invite is the grand introduct
with it.

Do those three articles on baby shower invitations really have useful, unique content without fluff? If I was critiquing this site, this would be the kind of thing I would be looking for on the sitemap as clues of content problems.

What about these two pages found on the same site:

Many companies now offer beautiful safari baby shower invitations.

Baby Shower Invitations For Twins
Double the blessing and a baby shower invitations for twins should convey the excitement.

Twin Baby Shower Invitation
A twin baby shower invitation has the added feat of acknowledging more than one gender.

The reason webmasters do this is not for the benefit of the visitor. It's for the benefit of the search engine. They hope that each page will rank well for its variation of the phrase, and therefore bring a lot more traffic to the site than just one article optimized for one of the phrases.

Today, this type of keyword focused content will get your site into trouble, so check through your sitemap to identify possible problems. You can combine similar articles into one, but make sure you cut the fluff and make these articles the best they can be.

- **Titles & headlines**

The <title> tag is an important part of a webpage as it tells the visitor what the page is about (the title is often used in Google as the anchor text to the page). The headline on the page is also important for similar reasons. Google has traditionally used keywords in the title and headlines to help rank a page, so yes, you guessed it, webmasters have abused these areas.

1. Your titles should be written for HUMANS, not search engines.
2. Your headlines should be written for HUMANS, not search engines (are you seeing a pattern here?).
3. Your title and headline should not be the same on any particular page.
4. No two pages should share the same title.

In the past, one of the best ways to rank a page for a particular phrase was to use the exact phrase for the title and the opening headline. Of course, the phrase would be sprinkled down the page as well, but the title and headline were strong ranking factors. Today, this won't work (at least for the long-term), so don't use a single keyword phrase as either the title or headline, or both. Titles and headlines should be crafted to draw the reader in. They can include topic-related phrases, but don't stuff, and above all, **write them for humans.**

While we are on the topic of page titles, make sure that no two pages on your site share the same title. This also goes for Meta descriptions if you use them. No two pages should contain the same Meta description, and that includes a "template" description that just substitutes a word or phrase each time it's used (as is typical on doorway pages).

• **Written for the search engine or the visitor?**

We've touched on this several times already, but it is so important that I am including it as a separate bullet point. Was the content written for a human or for the search engines? If the latter, or you are not sure, then that piece of content needs some work.

• **Hidden text on the page?**

One way that webmasters have tried to fool the search engines is with hidden text that contains keyword phrases. Hidden text can be achieved a few different ways, but perhaps the simplest is white text on a white background.

To check for hidden text, open the webpage in a browser and click on it somewhere. Now press CTRL+A (command + A on a Mac computer) to select all. Everything on the page will become selected, including anything that may be hidden. Check to make sure that all of text on the page is visible. Any hidden text that is found should be removed immediately.

• **Visible blocks of text that are only there for the search engines.**

An example of this is when a web page lists "incoming search terms", like this one:

Incoming search terms:

- food presentation ideas
- food presentation
- fruit decoration images
- funny food presentation
- fruit art with kids
- fruits foods pictures
- garnishing with vegetables
- picture of joke flower
- food wallpaper
- funny food garnish

What is the point of that list?

Does it in any way help the visitor?

Lists like this serve one purpose only – to add keywords to the page to try to make it rank better in Google. Therefore, according to Google, it is spam.

Incoming search term lists are not the only type of block you'll find on web pages. On travel sites, I've often seen long lists of towns or cities. They are often not hyperlinked to relevant sections of the site, so only serve to add keywords to a page.

Any block of text on your page that is only there to increase keywords on that page, really do need to be removed ASAP.

• **Over-optimization of the page as a whole.**

Google has gone out of its way to stop webmasters over-optimizing their sites because SEO is spoiling their otherwise great search results by showing pages that don't deserve to be at the top on merit.

While a lot of over-optimization relates to the backlinks of a website (and we'll cover that later), it also applies to what is on the website itself.

Take a look at the pages on your site and see whether a single phrase is used more than you might expect, thus making it obvious the phrase(s) was an intended target. If you find any, also check to see whether:

• Links to that page are using that phrase as anchor text?

• Is that phrase also in key areas of your web page, like title, meta description, H1 header, opening paragraph, ALT tag, image title tags, bolded, italic etc.

As a general rule, SEO should be "invisible".

I don't mean that there is none. Just that what is there should be discrete and not obvious and in-your-face.

There are WordPress plugins available that are designed to help check your on-page SEO. These are keyword driven checks and I think they are a bad idea. Content should NOT be keyword driven, it should be visitor driven.

If you have been using an SEO plugin that checks for placement of keywords in an article, I'd recommend using it to de-optimize your articles (removing phrases from places they really don't need to be) and once done, delete the plugin.

• **Is your content driven by keywords, or by what the visitors want?**

This is always a good check to make. Ask yourself whether the content you write on your site is driven by keyword research, or driven by what your visitors want.

I'm not saying you cannot use keywords in your content, of course you can. My point is this; instead of thinking you have to write an article about the phrase "tablet vs. laptop":

Keyword	Approximate CPC (Search) [?]
☐ tablet vs laptop ▼	€4.84

.. just because it commands a high cost per click, consider writing an article on "Advantages and disadvantages of using a tablet instead of a laptop".

OK, it could be the same article right? However, thinking about your content in terms of the visitor instead of your keyword research tool should ensure your content has a fighting chance of pleasing Google. Of course, you could include the phrase "tablet vs. laptop" in your article if you wanted (and it made sense to do so). I'm just suggesting a different approach to choosing the topics you write about. Think what article the visitor wants to see first, then go and see which keywords are relevant to the article.

• **Does your content reflect search/visitor intent?**

Does your web page offer a good match for the search terms it's found for?

In other words, if you rank #1 in Google for "natural pain killers", but your web page only mention one in passing while discussing an array of pharmaceutical pain killers, is the visitor going to be happy with your page? I doubt it. For starters, they wanted pain killers plural and secondly they wanted natural pain killers and your page is mostly about pharmaceutical pain killers.

As we've seen, Google have ways of measuring how happy visitors are with your page, like bounce rate, time on site, social signals, visitor interaction etc.

Therefore *it's important you don't try to rank for phrases that are a poor match for your content.*

• **Does your page provide something not already in the top 10?**

Does your content provide something that is not already available in the top 10 of Google? If not, why should it replace one of those pages in the top 10?

So what type of things can you add to your web page to make it stand out from the rest? What can you include that the other top 10 pages don't have?

Things like:

• Personal stories

• Your own opinion

• Your own unique thoughts, ideas etc.

• Images or photographs that work with the topic of your page.

• Visitor interaction – maybe a poll asking for visitor opinion. A poll coupled with an active comments section would create a great resource, especially if the topic of your page was a little controversial.

Content quality checklist

Look at every page on your website. The following checklist should be applied to your content.

• If the page is essentially an article, could it appear in a magazine?

• Is this the type of content that people would want to bookmark?

• Would people like to share this content with their friends and followers?

• Check a sentence or two in Google to see if your content has been used (illegally or otherwise) on other websites. If it has, you need to implement Google authorship immediately and hope Google gives you authorship of your content. Also, contact any webmaster that is illegally displaying your content and ask them to remove it (see the article I linked to in this section of the book on copyright infringement).

• If it's a product review, is it unbiased? Does it tell the good, the bad and the ugly? Does your review add information that gives opinions and views which are not found on the manufacturer's website, or any other website for that matter?

• If you use affiliate links, do your visitors know they are affiliate links? They should!

• Read each piece of content and look for keyword stuffing. Does it read naturally for a human, or was it written for a search engine? If any word or phrase appears more often than might be expected in a naturally written piece of content, then re-write it.

• How much fluff is in your article? Try to make sure your content does not contain fluff and filler. Get rid of any sentences that are only there to increase word count. If you have to remove a lot of fluff, perhaps the article could benefit from a total re-write.

• Do any two (or more) articles overlap in terms of what they talk about? Is the same information mentioned on more than one page of the site? If so, get rid of the duplication.

• Check your sitemap for possible problems. Are there any entries with similar filenames or titles that may indicate the articles cover the same/similar material? Are there any entries that suggest content was written around keywords rather than around the interests of the visitor? If so, get rid (or re-write) all content that was not written specifically for the visitors.

• Check all of your page titles and headlines to make sure that you don't use the same title and headline on any given piece of content. Headlines and titles should work together to entice the visitor. They should be written for the visitor and not for the search engines.

• Make sure you don't use the same title on more than one page.

• Check Meta descriptions if you use them. These should not be keyword stuffed, and again, should be written for the visitor to tell them what the content is about.

• Make sure you don't use the same Meta description (or "templated" description) on more than one page.

• Check each page for hidden text and remove any that you find.

• Are there any visible blocks of text on your pages that are only there for the search engines? If yes, get rid of them.

• SEO should be "invisible". Is it difficult to spot intentional SEO on your pages/site?

• Is your content driven by keywords or by what the visitor wants? Check... If it's the former, you need to clean up the content.

• Check to see what keywords your pages are being found for. Does your page reflect the searchers intent for these keywords?

• Does your page provide something not found on any other web page?

Checklist Point #10 – Inbound link profiles

Getting links back to your website has always been one of the main jobs for any webmaster. Although Google didn't like it, they did tolerate the behavior, at least until they rolled out their Penguin. Overnight, established websites dropped from the rankings. Pages that had been holding the top slot for years suddenly disappeared.

Google had done something that no-one believed they ever would. They started to enforce their guidelines relating to "link schemes".

> *"**Any links intended to manipulate a site's ranking** in Google search results may be **considered part of a link scheme**. This includes any behavior that manipulates links to your site, or outgoing links from your site. Manipulating these links may affect the quality of our search results, and as such **is a violation of Google's Webmaster Guidelines**."*

http://support.google.com/webmasters/bin/answer.py?hl=en&answer=66356

Any site that is seen to be participating in link schemes is in danger of ranking loss. However, even worse than that, any site that HAD participated in link schemes is also in danger. That means if you have a site that you are now running "by the book", but you had been involved in some dodgy link schemes in the past, your rankings could be seriously affected.

Google are looking for unnatural links. That is, links that have clearly been built by the webmaster, usually, though not always, on a large scale, and often of low quality.

To put it bluntly, **Google don't want you to build links to your own website**, at least not links whose sole purpose is to improve your rankings. As you look through your own backlink profile, it's important to be able to identify links that may be causing your site a problem and deal with them accordingly. These include any links that Google would consider part of a "link scheme".

Now, before I go through the kinds of links that will hurt your site, let me be clear about one thing. If your site received a penalty because of its backlinks, cleaning up those backlinks WILL NOT return your site to the same "pre-penalty" rankings. The reason is that your pre-penalty rankings were achieved WITH these spammy links, while they were still being counted by Google. These spammy links were helping your pages rank. Removing them means your pages don't have the same inbound links, and therefore won't rank as high. So, while cleaning up your links is vital to your long term success, don't expect that cleaning them up will put your old rankings back. For that, you'll need to build new, stronger, authority links to your site to replace the ones you've deleted/removed.

Ok, it's important to know what constitutes a bad link. Before we look at that though, it's probably better if I tell you how to find the links that point to your site.

Finding backlinks to your website

There are several tools you can use, some free, some paid. However, the one you should all be using as part of your backlink search is Google Webmaster Tools (which is free).

Google Webmaster Tools

Google webmaster tools (https://www.google.com/webmasters/tools/home?hl=en)

If you don't have an account with Google Webmaster Tools, you should get one. If Google wants to notify you of problems with your site (spiderability, spyware detected, links warnings, etc), they'll do it through Google Webmaster Tools (GWT).

GWT will show you the links that Google know about.

Just go to the **Traffic** section of the sidebar, and then select **Links to your site**:

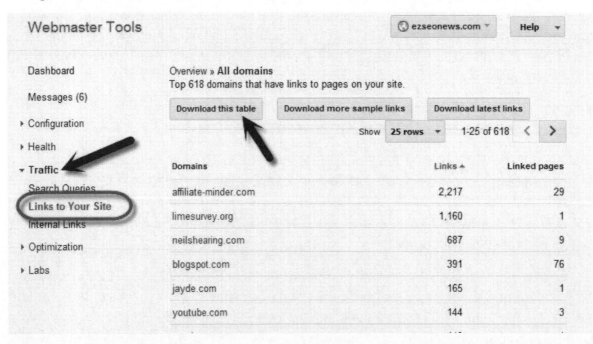

There is a link at the top of the table allowing you to download all of the links in the table. You'll get data on how many times a domain links to your site, and how many pages on your site it links to.

You can inspect the backlinks from any of these domains by clicking the hyperlink in the **Domains** column.

For example, in the list of domains pointing at my site, I didn't recognize a domain called **greenscapemedia.com.** I clicked the hyperlink to see what pages on my site it is linking to:

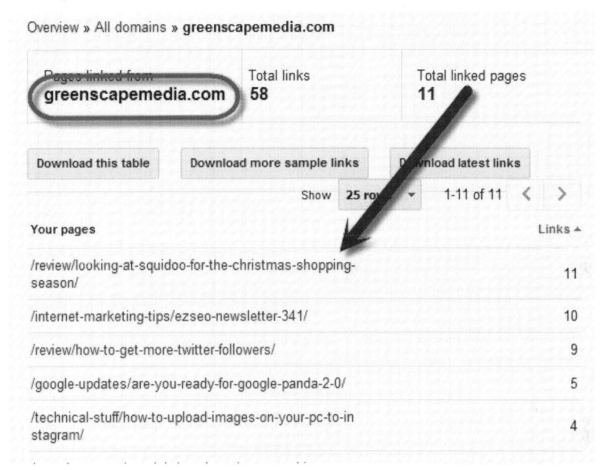

This page tells me that greenscapemedia.com has a total of 58 links to my site.

The table lists my pages that the domain links to, and how many links point to each of these pages.

I can see that greenscapemedia.com links to 11 of my pages in total (the table tells me it's showing 1-11 of 11 pages).

I can also see that this domain has 11 links pointing at the top URL, 10 pointing to the next, 9 to the next and so on (the links column on the right).

I can view the URLs on greenscapemedia.com that link to any of my pages by clicking the URL hyperlink (arrow in the screenshot) for my page. If I check the links pointing to my "Squidoo for Christmas Shopping" post, I can see:

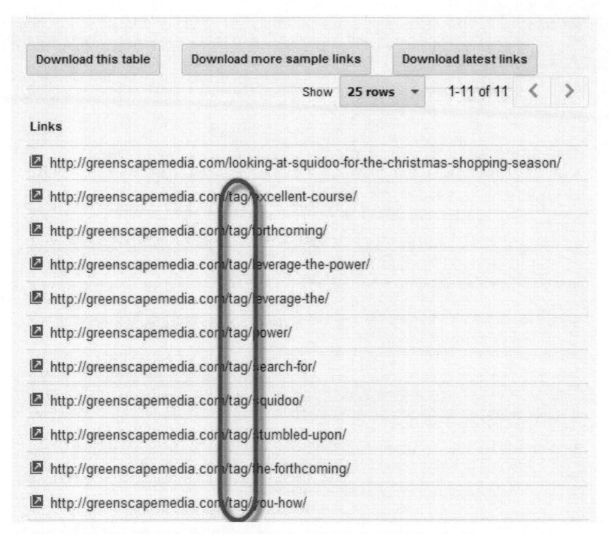

In this case, it looks like one "article" on greenscapemedia.com is linking to my page and the other 10 links are on tag pages. I'd guess that those tag pages are the various tags this webmaster used when tagging his main article. I can also see that this webmaster stole my title (and therefore probably part of my article).

I can click these hyperlinks to open these pages in my web browser. This allows me to view the links to my site.

The URL at the top of this list is basically a spam page and one that I would try to get removed if my site had been penalized for dodgy backlinks.

I should now go back and check the 10 other pages on my site that greenscapemedia.com is linking to.

What I love about GWT is that you get to see the link data that Google has for your website. I'm sure they probably don't show you everything, but it really is a great start to see their backlink data. GWT is always my first stop to find any problematic backlinks.

SEO Spyglass

SEO Spyglass is a commercial tool, though there is a free version to get you started. The free version won't let you save your data and there may be other limitations, but it can find links that aren't reported in GWT.

SEO Spyglass (http://www.link-assistant.com/seo-spyglass/)

Essentially, with SEO Spyglass, you type in the URL of your site and the software does the rest. It goes off to numerous sources to find backlinks to your website.

SEO Spyglass gives you masses of information about the links to your site. Things like:

- The URL that links to your site,
- Which page it links to,
- The anchor text,
- Whether the link it dofollow or nofollow,
- IP address,
- Domain age,
- How many links per page
- Lots, lots more.

SEO Spyglass really is a great tool for finding backlinks and link data for your site.

Ahrefs

This site is a popular one, for good reason. It does an excellent job of finding links to your website. The free version is very limited, so to get the best out of this tool, you need a paid subscription.

Ahrefs (http://ahrefs.com/)

Majestic SEO

Majestic SEO has a really useful free option and more comprehensive paid plans.

Majestic SEO (http://www.majesticseo.com/)

To see what is included for free, view this page:

http://blog.majesticseo.com/general/what-majesticseo-gives-you-for-free/

I'd recommend you sign up for a free account. Once you have done that, you can create a free Report for your domain. This involves uploading a text file to your server to prove the domain is yours. Once confirmed, Majestic SEO starts to analyze links to your domain. You'll then find the report in your reports screen. See the post above for a good introduction to using Majestic SEO. It includes an excellent video "webinar".

Ok, so you know now how to find the links, but how do you evaluate them?

Link schemes

Remember this quote from earlier?

> *"Any links intended to manipulate a site's ranking in Google search results may be considered part of a link scheme. This includes any behavior that manipulates links to your site, or outgoing links from your site. Manipulating these links may affect the quality of our search results, and as such is a violation of Google's Webmaster Guidelines."*

Link schemes include "any links intended to manipulate a site's ranking in Google search results".

Here are the schemes that can get you into trouble. You should check your site to make sure you are not engaging in these activities:

• **Buying or selling links that pass PageRank.** If your site has bought links, or sells links, then Google will probably come after you. Please note that when I say "buying", I don't necessarily mean that money changes hands. You could pay for a backlink in any number of ways – goods, services, free products, etc. If a webmaster has taken any kind of "reward" to host your links, then they are considered part of a link scheme. This even includes links found in product reviews, where you have given the webmaster a free copy of your product in exchange for the review and backlink.

• **Partner pages.** These were all the rage 10 years ago. You put up a partner page on your site and linked to other websites in return for a link back. These were also commonly called resource pages. Get rid of any links on a resource/partner page that are reciprocated (i.e., those sites that link back to yours).

• **Linking to undesirable neighborhoods.** If you link to any other site on the web, you are responsible for that link. Google sees links as votes for another website, so if you link to spammy websites, or even websites unrelated to your content, be warned, you could be penalized for it.

One of the places that webmasters unknowingly link to these bad neighborhoods is in the comments section of their website. When people leave comments, they often leave their URL, which could end up as an active link in the comments section on your website. Even if the link looks good now, there is nothing to stop the author of that comment redirecting it later to a porn site, or other undesirable website that you would not want to be associated with. Because of this, I'd recommend you make comment links nofollow. At least this way you are telling Google that you don't necessarily endorse that link.

• **Automated backlinks**. Backlinks built in an automated fashion using software and/or spun content will cause you problems. Not only are the backlinks generated by these tools of low quality, they are also fairly easy for search engines to identify. If you have backlinks built in this way, try your best to remove them.

• **Links in articles that you publish on other websites, where the anchor text is clearly trying to manipulate the rank of your web page.**

Here is an example that Google uses within their guidelines:

Links that are inserted into articles with little coherence, for example:
most people sleep at night. you can buy cheap blankets at shops. a blanket keeps you warm at night. you can also buy a wholesale heater. It produces more warmth and you can just turn it off in summer when you are going on france vacation.

See how the anchor texts within the body of this article are keyword phrases? These are clearly an attempt to manipulate rankings and Google will get you for it.

If you write articles for other sites (e.g. guest blogs), I'd recommend that you use a resource box at the end of the article, and link to your homepage using either the site name, or site URL as the anchor text. If you want to include a link within the body of the article, I'd suggest using either the URL of the page you are linking to, or its title/headline as the anchor text. These are far more natural than keyword-focused anchor text.

• **Low quality links in general, but Google specifically mentions low-quality directory and bookmark sites.**

I know there are a lot of tempting backlinking gigs on fivver.com, but don't use them. Once you have been submitted to hundreds of low quality directories or bookmark services, you won't be able to get those links taken down, so the damage is permanent.

Other types of low quality links include any type of "profile link" that is clearly only being used for the backlink.

Forum signature links are also bad for your rankings. If you are a member of a forum and you want to include a link to your site in your signature, use your site name or URL as the anchor text. Using a keyword phrase is clearly only trying to get your page to rank better for that keyword phrase.

- **Theme & widget backlinks.** In recent years, another link-building "loophole" was to create a template, or maybe a WordPress widget/plugin, that would be given away for free. Anyone using the theme or plugin would have a link inserted into their homepage (usually in the footer), back to the author's website. Google clamped down on this during 2012 and penalized a lot of websites.

- **Site-wide links.** We've talked about this earlier in the book. Any links that appear on all the pages of your site are called site-wide links. An example would be a blogroll on a WordPress site that usually lists "favorite blogs" in the sidebar. However, site-wide links have been abused by people buying them on other sites, so Google have hit them hard.

I know we all have navigation on our sites, and some items do get placed on every page of the site. However, pay particular attention to any site-wide links that use a keyword phrase as the anchor text. These are the ones that are more likely to get you into trouble. You know the ones – a "make money online" or "buy cheap contact lenses" link in the footer of all pages on your site. All site-wide links with keyword rich anchor text need to be looked at, and changed.

As you can see, link building has just become a lot more difficult. If you listen to Google, they'll just tell you to write great content and the links will come naturally. It's really not that simple because webmasters are not so generous about linking out to other websites. We therefore do need to find ways to get backlinks that at least appear to be more natural. My companion book "SEO 2013 & Beyond" has ideas for these (see appendix at the back for details of my other books).

In terms of critiquing/cleaning up your backlink profile, your job is to try to identify them and clean up ALL poor quality links pointing to your site. The job then is to build new, better quality links to replace them.

Make a list of all bad links to your site

You really do need to make a list of all bad links pointing to your site and then contact each webmaster in turn to ask them to remove the link. Successful or not (and in most cases it won't be), document every attempt you make. When you have the data to show you have tried to clean up your backlinks, you can then approach Google using their Disavow tool (https://www.google.com/webmasters/tools/disavow-links-main?pli=1).

The disavow tool tells Google that you want these links ignored AND that you have tried to clean them up. There are no guarantees with the disavow tool, but it is worth a go when you consider your final option, which is moving the site to a new domain and beginning the backlink process from scratch.

There is a good article here that describes one person's positive results using the disavow tool:

http://www.seomoz.org/ugc/googles-disavow-tool-works-penalty-removal

Other specific things to look out for in your backlink profile

1. **Diverse IPs** – Is there a good spread of IP addresses for the pages that link to your website? A lot of links from very similar IP addresses may indicate a blog network, or links from self-owned domains.
2. **Lots of links from the same domain** could indicate site-wide links that may need to be removed. If the site is authority and you get traffic from that site, then you might want to leave those links intact. If they are site-wide on low quality domains, then get them removed.
3. **Too many keyword phrase anchor texts.** Google Penguin is looking at the anchor text of inbound links. If you have a lot of links with the exact same anchor text, then is that natural? If it is the name of your site, then yes. If it is commercial keyword phrases that you want your site to rank for, then no. In 2012, anchor text links became a lot less important. My advice is to water these down significantly and aim for links designed to increase your authority, i.e., using your domain name, brand name or domain URL as the anchor text.
4. **Too many backlinks on low quality directories**. We mentioned this earlier.
5. **Backlinks from spun content**. This is a huge problem if you ever used automated backlink software to create backlinks using spun content. Spun content is one of the deadly sins of SEO and Google are on the warpath. They are getting better and better at detecting it, so if you find backlinks in spun content, do your best to get them taken down. Sometimes this type of backlink is easy to spot by looking at the titles of the pages containing the backlinks. Here is an example of backlinks I found in GWT for one site that clearly used spun content for backlinks:

Links

http://goarticles.com/article/Is-Serrapeptase-The-solution-to-Dupuytren-s-Disease/

http://goarticles.com/article/Serrapeptase-A-Feasible-Therapy-For-Numerous-Sclerosis/

http://goarticles.com/article/Serrapeptase-A-potential-Strategy-to-Multiple-Sclerosis/

http://goarticles.com/article/Utilizing-Serrapeptase-to-alleviate-Bodily-Discomfort/

This type of backlink is VERY bad for your site. Fortunately, these links were on the GoArticles website. I contacted them about the spammy nature of these articles and they took them down.

Inbound link profile checklist

Check the links pointing to your site using the tools mentioned in this book. If you only use one, I'd recommend GWT.

Have you participated in link schemes? This includes:

• Buying or selling links to pass Page Rank? Get rid of paid links.

• Do you have a partner / resources page on your site containing reciprocal links? Remove all links that are reciprocated.

• Are you linking (knowingly or unknowingly perhaps via the comments system) to bad neighborhoods? Get these links removed

• Do you have backlinks created by automated tools? Try to get these taken down.

• Are backlinks coming in from content that was spun? Try to get these taken down.

• Are the backlinks found in the body of articles linking to your site using keyword rich anchor text? If so, I'd recommend you change these keyword links and use your domain name, brand name, domain URL or title/headline of the article, as the link text.

• Are there any low quality directory or bookmarking links? These will cause you trouble so if you cannot remove them, they should be added to your list of links to disavow, if you eventually have to do that.

• Are there any backlinks to your site from themes or widgets that you have created? If so, you need to deactivate those links.

• Are there any links on your website that link out to other websites from themes or widgets you may be using? If so, remove them.

• Are there site-wide links pointing to your site from low quality websites? If so, they need to be removed. Site-wide links from high quality websites are probably OK, and I wouldn't remove those except as a last resort.

• Are your links from a diverse set of IP addresses? If not, get more links on different IP addresses.

• Do you have links from other websites you own? Are those links purely to help your pages rank better or is there a good reason to cross-link. If there is no good reason to cross-link the sites, remove those links.

• Are there lots of links from the same domain? If the domain is low quality, get them removed.

• Is there a high percentage of inbound links using keywords phrases you are targeting as anchor text? If so, I'd advise you to water these down. Include more links that use the domain/brand name, URL or title/headline of the content you are linking to.

Real-world examples of bad SEO

Modern SEO is not just about keeping the search engines happy, it's first and foremost about keeping your visitors happy. Their time on the site, including bounce rate and social interaction with your pages, are increasingly important signals that the search engines use to help decide how good your content is.

In this section, I want to highlight some examples of bad SEO that I found while critiquing a number of websites.

An example of bad navigation

This was the sidebar on the website:

There are 4 sections to this navigation bar and I should also mention that this was a WordPress site.

The first is the search box, which is a good thing, though this was the default WordPress search box which isn't much use.

Under that is a section labeled **"Pages"**. Pages in WordPress are one of two forms of content, the other being "Posts". This site seems to be mixing pages and posts in a way that makes me think the webmaster had no clear plan for the structure of the site. Either that, or the site was built initially with pages, but the webmaster wanted to add more content at a later date and so decided upon posts.

My own advice is to restrict the use of Pages in WordPress to the "legal pages" and use posts for all content written for the visitor. There are of course some exceptions, but this is a good general rule that allows you to make use of the excellent structural organization built into WordPress itself.

The next area of the navigation bar is an **"Archives"** section.

What is the purpose of this?

Does it help the visitor?

If this site was news based, where someone might like to check a news story from last month, then the archives section would be worth considering. However, this site isn't. In fact it's a fairly static site with little or no new content being added. Therefore the archive section just clutters an already cluttered navigation system.

The final area of the navigation menu is the **"Categories"** section. This is actually a useful section for visitors because they'll be able to find relevant POSTS. Note I put "posts" in capital letters, because PAGES won't be included in the category system (which only shows posts). Therefore the PAGES listed in the top section of the navigation menu won't be found using this category menu at the bottom.

You can see how the navigation system on this site is not very well organized and would only serve to confuse a visitor.

Things actually get worse. This website has a sitemap, which you can see here:

URL	Priority	Change Frequency	LastChange (GMT)
http:// /	100%	Daily	2011-11-18 23:36
http:// /medical-disclaimer/	30%	Weekly	2011-11-18 23:36
http:// /contact/	30%	Weekly	2011-11-18 23:36
http:// /how-to-treat-depression/	30%	Weekly	2011-11-10 23:57
http:// /help-for-depression/	30%	Weekly	2011-07-01 23:44
http:// /how-to-deal-with-depression/	30%	Weekly	2010-12-18 17:49
http:// /depression-treatment-centers/	30%	Weekly	2010-12-18 17:45
http:// /treatments-for-depression/	30%	Weekly	2010-12-18 17:32
http:// /privacy-policy/	30%	Weekly	2010-12-15 20:50

Generated with Google Sitemap Generator Plugin for WordPress by Arne Brachhold. This XSLT template is released under GPL.

The sitemap only has 9 entries, and that included the homepage and three "legal pages". Only 5 content pages were included, yet we can see from the sidebar navigation that this site did have 40+ posts and a few content pages.

A sitemap should list all important URLs on the site, most notably the posts. Disclaimers and other "legal" pages can be left off the sitemap. The main role of the sitemap is to make sure the search engines can find the important pages on your site.

Overall then, the navigation system on this site (which I believe has now been taken down since I originally critiqued it for the owner), is a good example of what not to do.

If you would like to test out your SEO sleuthing skills, have a look at the pages in the sidebar menu (Pages section) and see another major mistake that this site made. Hint: Look at the page titles.

An example of over-optimization

Have a look at this web page:

The webmaster was clearly trying to rank this page for "How to build a solar panel".

The Header section of this page used the text "How to build a solar panel" in an H1 header. Then there is an opening H1 header that has the same phrase (that's two H1 headers on the same page which is never good). The exact same phrase then appears twice more and this is all ABOVE THE FOLD. This phrase is also in the title tag of the page, plus the Meta description of the page. It is also found in the ALT text of an image on the page.

This is an extreme example of over-optimization.

Example of fake comments

Here are the comments on a website I was critiquing:

1. R. Vest on Thu, 4th Nov 2010 10:08 am

   Materials used to construct this product are very good.

   I use it to keep a 12 Volt battery charged.

   It is being used with a Brunton 12 volt solar controller.
   Rating: 4 / 5

2. M. Sant on Thu, 4th Nov 2010 12:07 pm

   This is an excellent panel at a great price. I use it with a HQRP solar controller and a Walmart 115ah deepcycle marine battery and couldn't be more pleased.
   Rating: 5 / 5

3. Gayla Hieber on Thu, 4th Nov 2010 1:37 pm

   It keeps my batteries charged up in my camper so I can keep cell phone charged up and reading lights on at night.
   Rating: 5 / 5

4. J Galt II on Thu, 4th Nov 2010 2:23 pm

   Well-made solar panel, well-packed for shipping. I am very satisfied with this purchase and spent some time looking into and finding what I wanted. It is placed on dash of my RV and used to maintain my batteries away from AC power source.

   Quite reassuring to have Amazon as a partner in transactions... excellent value. It works great.

   Rating: 5 / 5

Notice that all of the comments were on the same day within 4 hours of each other? That in itself is not unheard of, but the comments themselves made me suspicious because they each included a rating out of 5 (and none of them had Gravatar images).

To check the comments, I took a sentence from one of them and searched Google for that sentence (in quotes):

"It keeps my batteries charged up in my camper so I can keep cell phone cl

Web   Images   Maps   Shopping   More ▾   Search tools

15 results (0.36 seconds)

Ad related to "It keeps my batteries charged up in my camper so I ... ⓘ
Ask an RV Tech Online - Technicians Will Answer in Minutes
rv.justanswer.com/Camper-RV
Questions Answered Every 9 Seconds.
Lawyer - Doctor - Nurse - Veterinarian

Amazon.com: Customer Reviews: HQRP 20W Mono-crystalline ...
www.amazon.com/HQRP-Mono-crystalline.../B002HT09TO
It keeps my batteries charged up in my camper so I can keep cell phone
charged up and reading lights on at night. Help other customers find the most
helpful ...

Amazon.com: HQRP 20W Mono-crystalline Solar Panel 20 Watt 12 ...
www.amazon.com › ... › Solar & Wind Power › Solar Panels
It keeps my batteries charged up in my camper so I can keep cell phone
charged up and reading lights on at night. Published on March 19, 2010 by Gayla ...

Amazon.com: Gayla Hieber's review of HQRP 20W Mono-crystalline ...
www.amazon.com/review/RW67BDW88G8WU
It keeps my batteries charged up in my camper so I can keep cell phone
charged up and reading lights on at night. Gayla Hieber March 19, 2010. Overall:
5.0 out ...

Looking for customer reviews for HQRP 20W Mono-crystalline Solar ...
askville.amazon.com › ... › Shopping › Lawn Garden
2 answers - 8 Jun 2011
It keeps my batteries charged up in my camper so I can keep cell phone
charged up and reading lights on at night. 4 of 4 found the following ...

Google found that exact same sentence /comment on 15 web pages, including Amazon.

Could the webmaster have found these comments on Amazon and added them to his website? Or maybe he paid someone to add comments and they copied them from Amazon?

Whatever the answer, this is bad.

I checked the other "fake" comments on the webpage and every one of them was found on numerous other websites including Amazon.

Example of sneaky affiliate links

There is nothing wrong with having affiliate links on your website. However, visitors should know that they are affiliate links, and "hidden" affiliate links designed to set a cookie are not a good idea.

One site I critiqued a while ago used the whole of the background of his site (i.e. all the space to the left and right of the main content) as one big affiliate link. Click on the background ANYWHERE and you were directed via an affiliate link to the merchant site. This clearly is not a good idea. As I was critiquing the site I cannot remember how many times I ended up on the merchant site. I can only guess at how annoyed visitors got with this. That was an extreme case.

Here is another case of hidden affiliate links:

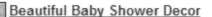

On this page, the webmaster had hyperlinked all of the images to Amazon with an affiliate link. The landing page was an Amazon search results page for the phrase **baby shower invitations**.

Why do this?

Does it in some way help the visitor?

Or is it an attempt to set a cookie on Amazon?

Of course, it could have been a genuine mistake, but this type of thing is not adding to the visitor experience.

An example of how NOT to create a contact us page

On the contact page of one affiliate site I critiqued, I found this:

Contact Information

If you have any questions about satellite TV systems or service, please call DISH Network or DIRECTV's toll-free telephone number, or click on the link listed below.

DISH Network

For questions about DISH Network satellite tv systems or service, contact U.S. Dish:

By phone: 1-888-228-0942

Online: Click here for U.S. Dish online support

DIRECTV

For questions about DIRECTV satellite TV systems or service, contact U.S. Direct:

By phone: 1-866-529-6828

Online: Click here for U.S. Direct online support

Instead of contact details for the site, it provided contact details of two merchants instead. That means visitors have no way to contact the webmaster of this website.

It also makes it look like this webmaster is pretending to be the merchant (or a website owned by the merchant).

Your contact page should give your visitors YOUR contact details so they can contact YOU! This not only builds trust, but is also a basic requirement of doing business online.

Incidentally, the same website also had a link in their menu labeled "Affiliate Information". This is typically only something found on a merchant site. On the Affiliate Information page, this website linked to the affiliate programs of the two merchants!

Example of a bad inbound link profile

Deciding what is a good or bad inbound link profile is quite a challenge, I mean what does a natural profile look like. How about this one:

Webpage PageRank	▾ %
PR: —	96.3% (1134)
PR: 1	1.6% (19)
PR: 0	0.8% (10)
PR: 3	0.8% (10)
PR: 2	0.3% (4)
PR: 4	0.0% (0)
PR: 5	0.0% (0)

There are links fromPR1, PR2 and PR3 pages, which is good. However, these amount to just 2.7% of all inbound links. A whopping 96.3% of inbound links (that's 1134 links) came from web pages where the Page Rank was N/A (the lowest possible rank, often found on very new pages, pages that have been penalized or pages of very poor quality).

This profile indicates to me that the webmaster went for quantity, not quality, and from some very poor sources. I'd expect to see this type of profile on a site that used automated backlinking software. This is exactly the type of thing that Google Penguin will bite you for.

Example of bad internal linking

Internal linking of pages on a website is done to help the visitor. Done correctly, it can help guide visitors to more information about certain topics.

On one website I critiqued, something strange was going on with the internal linking. Here are two examples of the type of internal linking I found:

ccount while others w only apply
'es actual dollars for the **consumer**.

Finding the best credit card de for your spe
credit cards can often be a mplicated, confu
have little or **no experience** managing cards.

The anchor text in the first example was "consumer", and the anchor text in the second example was "no experience".

When you internally link pages on your site using contextual links, the anchor texts MUST be related to the page you are linking to. The anchor text must also be fairly self-serving, not leaving anything to the imagination as to what the destination is about. I mean, what would a visitor think the destination URL is about if the link text is "consumer"? What about "no experience"?

The "consumer" link went to an article on "mileage credit cards".

The "no experience" link went to a page on "credit card debt relief".

Do these help the visitor? Nope! The only point I can think of is that the webmaster was trying to make sure their pages were crawled and indexed (and Page Rank passed around), so added more links to them in this way.

Here is another one:

> reveal a **secret weapon** that you can use aga
> cuss this strategy, let us just look briefly at th
> companies to recruit you as their customer.

What has "secret weapon" got to do with any article on credit cards?

Do you see the problem with these?

One final example on this site is this internal link:

> ## 6. Borrow against your 401k
>
> When you **take a loan against your 401k** you are paying
> your goal is a one time payoff of credit card debt it can
> than to throw away 29% interest to a credit lending insti

The anchor text "take a loan against your 401k" linked to a page that did not include the word 401K!

Where to go from here

"Make sure that your site adds value. Provide unique and relevant content that gives users a reason to visit your site first".

In 2012, SEO changed forever. Google became far less tolerant of activities that they see as rank manipulation. Google want to serve web pages that offer their visitors the best possible experience, and that means your primary focus should be on your Visitor. Not Google, not a keyword research tool, and certainly not automated tools that claim to do your SEO for you.

As webmasters, we have been given a choice. Stick to Google's rules, or lose out on free traffic from the world's biggest search engine.

Sure, there will always be someone advertising the next greatest "loophole" to beat the system, and they'll even have examples to prove their loophole works. These examples may even go against everything that Google wants and break all the rules, which will make them tempting to some. However, these loopholes are short-lived. My advice to you is to ignore anyone that tries to sell you a loophole, a trick, or anything else that is "under Google's radar". If you want long-lasting results, stick to the rules - Google's rules.

The SEO in this book (and in my SEO 2013 & Beyond Kindle book) is the SEO I use on a daily basis. It's the SEO I teach my students, and it's the SEO that I know works. For those that embrace the recent changes, SEO has actually become easier as we no longer have to battle against other sites whose SEO was done 24/7 by an automated tool or army of cheap labor. Those sites have largely been removed, and that levels the playing field nicely.

I assume you bought this book to help you clean up a site of your own. Just go through the checklist included at the end of this book, working your way through the points.

Oh, and good luck!

Appendix - The checklist

Checkpoint 1 - The domain name

• Exact Match Domain (EMD)? If yes, then be aware that this will work against you and you'll need to de-optimize the site for the phrase in the domain name.

• Keyword stuffed? There isn't much you can do with this other than move the site to a better domain. Keyword stuffed domains look spammy and don't instill much confidence in visitors. Unless there is good reason to keep the domain (like it still makes good income or ranks well), I'd consider moving the site to a better, brandable domain.

• Has your domain never ranked properly? If not, then check its history at the Way Back Machine. Consider a reconsideration request at Google if it looks like the domain was used before.

Checkpoint 2 - Web page real estate

• Resize your browser to 1024x768 and see what loads above the fold. Is there useful content? Are there too many adverts? If there are too many ads, especially above the fold, consider removing (or moving) them.

• If you removed all of the adverts from the pages on your site, would those pages still offer the visitor what they are looking for? If not, then the content is not good enough.

• Does your site have sneaky links in the footer, especially keyword rich anchor text links to your own site or an external site? If so, get rid of them.

Checkpoint 3 - site structure

• Is your navigation intuitive?

• Are all of the pages on your site just one or two clicks away from the homepage?

• Do you have site-wide links in the sidebar?

• Do you have site-wide links in the header?

• Do you have site-wide links in the footer?

NOTE: Site-wide links with keyword-rich anchor text are the most potentially damaging.

• If you have a large site, do you use dynamic menus, which change depending on the section of the site the visitor is viewing?

• Do you have a search box? If it is a WordPress default search box, I highly recommend you switch to a more efficient script, e.g. Google's custom search.

• Do you internally link the pages of your website from within the body of your content, not just via the navigation menus or a related posts menu?

• Is your content organized logically into "silos" where all related content is in the same category or folder? If necessary (e.g. on a large site), do you use sub-folders to help make the navigation more intuitive?

• If you are using WordPress, do you have tags that are only used once or twice? If so, remove them.

• If you are using WordPress, do you have tags that are identical to some of your categories? Never use a phrase for a tag if it is being used (or will be used) as a category.

Checkpoint 4 – Comments

• Does your website have a comments section where visitors can leave their own thoughts and questions?

• Does your website have a Contact Us form?

• If you have comments enabled, are you manually approving all comments? You should be.

• Check through all of the comments on your site and remove any fake or spam comments. In fact, remove any comment whose sole purpose is to get a backlink to a website.

• Make comment links nofollow.

• Going forward, only approve legitimate comments where it is clear the visitor read your content and added to the conversation with their insight.

Checkpoint 5 - Social presence

• Does the website have a presence on Facebook?

• Does the website have a presence on Twitter?

• Does the website have a presence on Google plus?

• Does your website have social sharing buttons that allow your visitors to share your content with their social media followers? You should include Twitter, Facebook and Google plus as a bare minimum.

• Setup Google Authorship for your site and connect your content to your Google plus profile.

Checkpoint 6 - Would you trust this site?

• Does the site have a photo of the webmaster/author of the content?

• Does your site have an About Us page?

• Are Comments enabled?

• Does your site pretend to be a merchant?

• Is the author of your site a recognized authority in the niche/industry?

• Are you using a Gravatar set up on the email address you use for your site?

• Is your business address displayed on the site, preferably with a phone number?

• When was the last time your site was updated?

• If appropriate, are there testimonials, and are they up to date?

• Is the copyright notice on your website the correct year?

• Do you display any trust symbols (if appropriate)

• Check all content for spellings and grammatical errors. Check your navigation systems for these errors as well.

• Are there unanswered comments on your site?

Checkpoint 7 - Bounce rates & time on site

I recommend you install the updated code here (which will give you a more accurate measurement of these parameters):

http://briancray.com/posts/time-on-site-bounce-rate-get-the-real-numbers-in-google-analytics/

Once installed and allowed to run for a few weeks, check your bounce rate and time on site at Google Analytics.

• Are your average bounce rates high?

• Are visitors spending a long or short time on your site?

• Look for specific pages where bounce rate is high AND time on site is low. Try to work out why these pages are suffering and fix them.

Checkpoint 8 - Legal pages

Not all of these pages are necessary for all types of website, so check which pages your site needs and add them if they are missing.

• Do you have a privacy page?

- Do you have a disclaimer page?

- Do you have a terms page?

- Do you have a contact page?

- Do you have an about us page?

- Do you have a medical disclaimer page?

- Do you have an email policy page?

- Do you have an outbound link policy page?

Checkpoint 9 - Content quality

Look at every page on your website. The following checklist should be applied to your content.

- If the page is essentially an article, could it appear in a magazine?

- Is this the type of content that people would want to bookmark?

- Would people like to share this content with their friends and followers?

- Check a sentence or two in Google to see if your content has been used (illegally or otherwise) on other websites. If it has, you need to implement Google authorship immediately and hope that Google gives you authorship of your own content. Also, contact any webmaster that is illegally displaying your content and ask them to remove it (see the article I linked to in this section of the book on copyright infringement).

- If it's a product review, is it unbiased? Does it tell the good, the bad and the ugly? Does your review add information, opinion and views that are not found on the manufacturer's website, or any other website for that matter?

- If you use affiliate links, do your visitors know they are affiliate links? They should!

- Read each piece of content and look for keyword stuffing. Does it read naturally for a human, or was it written for a search engine? If any word or phrase appears more often that might be expected in a naturally written piece of content, then re-write it.

- How much fluff is in your article? Try to make sure your content does not contain fluff and filler. Get rid of any sentences that are only there to increase word count. If you have to remove a lot of fluff, perhaps the article could benefit from a total re-write.

- Do any two (or more) articles overlap in terms of what they talk about? Is the same information mentioned on more than one page of the site? If so, get rid of the duplication.

• Check your sitemap for possible problems. Are there any entries with similar filenames or titles that may indicate the articles cover the same/similar material? Are there any entries that suggest content was written around keywords rather than around the interests of the visitor? If so, get rid (or re-write) all content that was not written specifically for the visitors.

• Check all of your page titles and headlines to make sure that you don't use the same title and headline on any given piece of content. Headlines and titles should work together to entice the visitor. They should be written for the visitor and not for the search engines.

• Make sure you don't use the same title on more than one page.

• Check Meta descriptions if you use them. These should not be keyword stuffed, and again, should be written for the visitor to tell them what the content is about.

• Make sure you don't use the same Meta description (or "templated" description) on more than one page.

• Check each page for hidden text and remove any that you find.

• Are there any visible blocks of text on your pages that are only there for the search engines? If so, get rid of them.

• SEO should be "invisible". Can you spot obvious attempts at SEO on your pages/site?

• Is your content driven by keywords or by what the visitor wants? Check... If it's the former, you need to clean up the content.

• Check to see what keywords your pages are being found for. Does your page reflect the searchers intent for these keywords?

• Does your page provide something not found on any other web page?

Checkpoint 10 - Inbound link profiles

Check the links pointing to your site using the tools mentioned in this book. If you only use one, I'd recommend Google Webmaster Tools (GWT).

Have you participated in link schemes? This includes:

• Buying or selling links to pass Page Rank? Get rid of paid links.

• Do you have a partner / resources page on your site containing reciprocal links? Remove all links that are reciprocated.

• Are you linking (knowingly or unknowingly perhaps via the comments system) to bad neighborhoods? Get these links removed

• Do you have backlinks created by automated tools? Try to get these taken down.

• Are backlinks coming in from content that was spun? Try to get these taken down.

• Are the backlinks found in the body of articles linking to your site using keyword rich anchor text? If so, I'd recommend you change these keyword links and use your domain name, brand name, domain URL or title/headline of the article as the link text.

• Are there any low quality directory or bookmarking links? These will cause you trouble and if you cannot remove them, they should be added to your list of links to disavow, if you eventually have to do that.

• Are there any backlinks to your site from themes or widgets that you have created? If so, you need to deactivate those links.

• Are there any links on your website that link out to other websites from themes or widgets you may be using? If so, remove them.

• Are there site-wide links pointing to your site from low quality websites? If so, they need to be removed. Site-wide links from high quality websites are probably OK, and I wouldn't remove those except as a last resort.

• Are your links from a diverse set of IP addresses? If not, get more links on different IP addresses.

• Do you have links from other websites you own? Are those links purely to help your pages rank better or is there a good reason to cross-link. If there is no good reason to cross-link the sites, remove those links.

• Are there lots of links from the same domain? If the domain is low quality, get them removed.

• Is there a high percentage of inbound links using keywords phrases you are targeting as anchor text? If so, I'd advise you to water these down. Include more links that use the domain/brand name, URL or title/headline of the content you are linking to.

Please leave a review on Amazon

If you enjoyed this book, PLEASE leave a review on the Amazon website. You can find the book listing here:

US: http://www.amazon.com/dp/B00BXFAULK

UK: https://www.amazon.co.uk/dp/B00BXFAULK

For all other Amazon stores, search for the book by B00BXFAULK

All the best

Andy Williams

More information from Dr. Andy Williams

If you would like more information, tips, tutorials or advice, there are two resources you might like to consider.

The first is my free weekly newsletter over at ezSEONews.com offering tips, tutorials and advice to online marketers and webmasters. Just sign up and my newsletter, plus SEO articles, will be delivered to your inbox. I cannot always promise a weekly schedule, but I do try ;)

I also run a course over at CreatingFatContent.com, where I build real websites in front of members in "real-time" using my system of SEO.

My other Kindle books

All of my books are available as Kindle books and paperbacks. You can view them all here:

http://amazon.com/author/drandrewwilliams

Here are a few of my more popular books:

Creating Web Content

Creating "Fat" Content that can rank and stick in Google

Google want to show the best web pages to their users, but what constitutes the "best"?

The answer is quite simple - the best content is the content that the visitors want to see.

Not very helpful? Then read this book. It's packed with advice on what Google actually want, and how you can deliver it with a simple mindset shift - by thinking in terms of "share-bait". That is, content that your visitors want to share with their friends, family and followers. Share-bait will put you on the right path to delivering content that keeps your visitors and search engines happy. It will give you an unfair advantage as your content has a better chance of not only ranking well, but sticking in the search engines.

Creating Web Content is a book packed with ideas, tips and strategies, for creating the most captivating, inspiring and fascinating content for your web site. By keeping your visitors happy, you won't have to worry about search engine algorithm changes, or Google slaps. The search engines will want to show your content to their users.

Search Amazon for **BOOLTZMERM**

Rapid Wordpress Websites

A visual step-by-step guide to building Wordpress websites fast!

Did you ever wish there was a tutorial that would show you just what you needed to know to create your first Wordpress website, without having to wade through stuff you'll never use?

Well this book is that tutorial. It teaches you on a strictly "need-to-know" basis, and will have you building your own website in hours. And I don't leave you stranded either. I created a companion website for readers of this book, with tutorials and help to take your Wordpress skills to the next level, when, and only when, YOU are ready.

What's in this book?

We start at the very beginning by getting good, reliable web hosting and choosing a domain name. I actually walk you through every step, so there will be no confusion.

Once you have your domain, we'll install Wordpress and have a look around the Wordpress Dashboard - think of this as your mission control.

After planning what we want to do, we'll actually build the companion site as we work through the book. We cover the essential settings in Wordpress that you need to know, how to use the editor, the difference between pages and post, categories and tags, etc.

We'll set up custom navigation so your visitors can find their way around your Wordpress site, and carefully use widgets to enhance the design and user experience.

Once the site is built, we'll play around with customizing the look and feel using themes, and I'll point you in the direction of some interesting plugins you might like to look at. These will be covered in more depth on the companion website.

The book will take you from nothing to a complete website in hours, and I'll point out a number of beginner mistakes and things to avoid.

Search Amazon for **B00JGWW86W**

Wordpress for Beginners

Do you want to build a website but scared it's too difficult?

Building a website was once the domain of computer geeks. Not anymore. WordPress makes it possible for anyone to create and run a professional looking website

While WordPress is an amazing tool, the truth is it does have a steep learning curve, even if you have built websites before using different tools. Therefore, the goal of this book is to take anyone, even a complete beginner, and get them building a professional looking website. I'll hold your hand, step-by-step, all the way.

As I was planning this book, I made one decision early on. I wanted to use screenshots of everything so that the reader wasn't left looking for something on their screen that I was describing in text. This book has plenty of screenshots. I haven't counted them all, but it must be close to 300. These images will help you find the things I am talking about. They'll help you check your settings and options against the screenshot of mine. You look, compare, and move on to the next section.

With so many screenshots, you may be concerned that the text might be a little on the skimpy side. No need to worry there. I have described every step of your journey in great detail. In all, this publication has over 35,000 words.

This book will surely cut your learning curve associated with WordPress.

Every chapter of the book ends with a "Tasks to Complete" section. By completing these tasks, you'll not only become proficient at using WordPress, but you'll become confident & enjoy using it too.

Search Amazon for **B009ZVO3H6**

Wordpress SEO

On-Page SEO for your Wordpress Site

Most websites (including blogs) share certain features that can be controlled and used to help (or hinder, especially with Google Panda & Penguin on the loose) with the on-site SEO. These features include things like the page title, headlines, body text, ALT tags and so on. In this respect, most sites can be treated in a similar manner when we consider on-site SEO.

However, different platforms have their own quirks, and WordPress is no exception. Out-of-the-box WordPress doesn't do itself any SEO favours, and can in fact cause you ranking problems, especially with the potentially huge amount of duplicate content it creates. Other problems include static, site-wide sidebars and footers, automatically generated meta tags, page load speeds, SEO issues with Wordpress themes, poorly constructed navigation, badly designed homepages, potential spam from visitors, etc. The list goes on.

This book shows you how to set up an SEO-friendly Wordpress website, highlighting the problems, and working through them with step-by-step instructions on how to fix them.

By the end of this book, your WordPress site should be well optimized, without being 'over-optimized' (which is itself a contributing factor in Google penalties).

Search Amazon for: **B00ECF70HU**

Kindle Publishing

Format, Publish & Promote your books on Kindle

Why Publish on Amazon Kindle?

Kindle publishing has captured the imagination of aspiring writers. Now, more than at any other time in our history, an opportunity is knocking. Getting your books published no longer means sending out hundreds of letters to publishers and agents. It no longer means getting hundreds of rejection letters back. Today, you can write and publish your own books on Amazon Kindle without an agent or publisher.

Is it Really Possible to Make a Good Income as an Indie Author?

The fact that you are reading this book description tells me you are interested in publishing your own material on Kindle. You may have been lured here by promises of quick riches. Well, I have good news and bad. The bad news is that publishing and profiting from Kindle takes work and dedication. Don't just expect to throw up sub-par material and make a killing in sales. You need to produce good stuff to be successful at this. The good news is that you can make a very decent living from writing and publishing on Kindle.

My own success with Kindle Publishing

As I explain at the beginning of this book, I published my first Kindle book in August 2012, yet by December 2012, just 5 months later, I was making what many people consider being a full time income. As part of my own learning experience, I setup a Facebook page in July 2012 to share my Kindle publishing journey (there is a link to the Facebook page inside this book). On that Facebook page, I shared the details of what I did, and problems I needed to overcome. I also shared my growing income reports, and most of all, I offered help to those who asked for it. What I found was a huge and growing audience for this type of education, and ultimately, that's why I wrote this book.

What's in this Book?

This book covers what I have learned on my journey and what has worked for me. I have included sections to answer the questions I myself asked, as well as those questions people asked me. This book is a complete reference manual for successfully formatting, publishing & promoting your books on Amazon Kindle. There is even a section for non-

US publishers because there is stuff there you specifically need to know. I see enormous potential in Kindle Publishing, and in 2013 I intend to grow this side of my own business. Kindle publishing has been liberating for me and I am sure it will be for you too.

Search Amazon for **B00BEIX34C**

Self-Publishing on Createspace

Convert & Publish your books on Createspace

Self-publishing your own work is easier than at any time in our history. Amazon's Kindle platform and now Createspace allow us to self-publish our work, with zero costs up front.

Createspace is a fantastic opportunity for writers. You publish your book, and if someone buys it, Createspace print it and send it to the customer. All the author needs to do is wait to be paid. How's that for hands-free and risk-free publishing?

This book takes you step-by-step through my own process for publishing. Topics covered include:

- Basic Text Formatting
- Which Font?
- Links and formatting checks
- Page Numbering in Word
- Adding a new title to Createspace
- Price calculator and deciding on Trim size
- Image DPI requirements
- Paint Shop Pro conversion process
- Common formatting problems
- Book Cover Templates
- Creating the cover with Photoshop Elements
- Creating the cover in Paint Shop Pro
- Submitting the book & cover to Createspace
- Expanded Distribution?

The book also includes links to a number of video tutorials created by the author to help you understand the formatting and submission process.

Search Amazon for **B00HG0GE0C**

CSS for Beginners

Learn CSS with detailed instructions, step-by-step screenshots and video tutorials showing CSS in action on real sites

Most websites and blogs you visit use cascading style sheets (CSS) for everything from fonts selection & formatting, to layout & design. Whether you are building WordPress sites or traditional HTML websites, this book aims to take the complete beginner to a level where they are comfortable digging into the CSS code and making changes to their own site. This book will show you how to make formatting & layout changes to your own projects quickly and easily.

The book covers the following topics:

- Why CSS is important
- Classes, Pseudo Classes, Pseudo Elements & IDs
- The Float property
- Units of Length
- Using DIVs
- Tableless Layouts, including how to create 2-column and 3-column layouts
- The Box Model
- Creating Menus with CSS
- Images & background images

The hands on approach of this book will get YOU building your own Style Sheets from scratch. Also included in this book:

- Over 160 screenshots and 20,000 words detailing ever step you need to take.
- Full source code for all examples shown.
- Video Tutorials.

The video tutorials accompanying this book show you:

- How to investigate the HTML & CSS behind any website.
- How to experiment with your own design in real time, and only make the changes permanent on your site when you are ready.

A basic knowledge of HTML is recommended, although all source code from the book can be downloaded and used as you work through the book.

Search Amazon for **B00AFV44NS**

Migrating to Windows 8.1

For computer users without a touch screen, coming from XP, Vista or Windows 7

Review: "What Microsoft should buy and give away now to drive sales"

New PCs are coming pre-installed with Windows 8, Microsoft's new incarnation of the popular operating system. The problem is, the PCs it is installed on are not usually equipped with the piece of hardware that Windows 8 revolves around - a touch screen.

Windows 8 is probably the least user-friendly version of the operating system ever released. It's almost like two different operating systems merged together. From the lack of a start menu, to features that only really make sense on a tablet or phone, Windows 8 has a lot of veteran Windows users scratching their heads. If you are one of them, then this book is for you.

After a quick tour of the new user interface, the book digs deeper into the features of Windows 8, showing you what everything does, and more importantly, how to do the things you used to do on older versions of Windows. The comprehensive "How to" section answers a lot of the questions new users have, and there's also a complete keyboard shortcut list for reference.

If you are migrating to Windows 8 from XP, Vista or Windows 7, then this book may just let you keep your hair as you learn how to get the most out of your computer. Who knows, you may even get to like Windows 8.

Search Amazon for **B00CJ8AD9E**

More Information from Dr. Andy Williams

If you would like more information, tips, tutorials or advice, there are two resources you might like to consider.

The first is my free weekly newsletter over at ezSEONews.com offering tips, tutorials and advice to online marketers and webmasters. Just sign up and my newsletter plus SEO articles will be delivered to your inbox. I cannot always promise a weekly schedule, but I try ;)

I also run a course over at CreatingFatContent.com, where I build real websites in front of members in "real-time" using my system of SEO.

Printed in Great Britain
by Amazon.co.uk, Ltd.,
Marston Gate.